*Flowers are a gift from God; unfortunately, he doesn't arrange them. In church, flower arrangements give life to the surroundings, connecting and bringing the congregation into harmony with the inanimate wood, stone and glass. Flower arranging is a science as well as an art, and there is an undeniable element of mystery: How do they do that?*

*Finally, nationally renowned flower-arranging expert Gay Estes has created an illustrated primer that demystifies the art of church flower arranging. From the Alpha to the Omega, here are practical instructions that will enable you to create divinely beautiful floral displays. You'll find detailed and illustrated information on every aspect of arranging: mechanics, containers, conditioning, using fresh and dried flowers, design principles, flower symbolism, the church year, floral traditions and colors, recycling, being frugal and, most importantly, enjoying it every step of the way.*

*Whether you are a novice or an experienced arranger—in or out of church—**The Church Ladies Guide to Divine Flower Arrangements** will provide you with real inspiration.*

THE CHURCH LADIES'
*Guide to*

# divine flower arranging

2365 Rice Boulevard, Suite 202, Houston, Texas   77005

Library of Congress Cataloging-in-Publication Data

Estes, Gay, 1937-
The church ladies' guide to divine flower arranging / by Gay Estes.
p. cm.
Includes bibliographical references.
ISBN 978-1-933979-29-8 (softcover : alk. paper)
1. Flower arrangement in churches.  I. Title.

SB449.5.C4E78 2008
745.92'6--dc22

2008018769

Book Design by Tutu Somerville
Printed in China through Asia Pacific Offset

# THE CHURCH LADIES'
## *Guide to*

# divine flower arranging

*Written and Illustrated by*
## GAY ESTES

**bright sky press**
HOUSTON AND ALBANY, TEXAS

# a CHURCH ARRANGER'S PRAYER

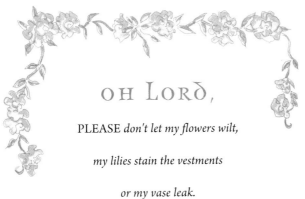

## OH LORD,

PLEASE *don't let my flowers wilt,*

*my lilies stain the vestments*

*or my vase leak.*

MAY *the Altar Guild not fight*

*over who gets to do the altar*

*and who must do the pews.*

LET *my arrangement neither fall,*

*nor catch fire from the candles.*

## AMEN

# taBLe of contents

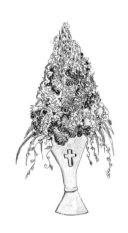

# aLpнa:
## IN THE BEGINNING

It is joyful to decorate a church. Where else can we literally place our gift upon the altar? The architecture and decorative details, altar hangings and stained glass burst with floral motifs, both naturalistic and stylized. The trees, vines, fruits, grains and flowers in religious art symbolize and remind us of life cycles.

Church flowers give life to the surroundings, connecting and bringing the congregation into harmony with the inanimate wood, stone and glass: a fresh reminder of the age-old traditions. Flowers are renewable, fresh and ever-changing.

My intention is to inform with a light touch. There is a saying in the Talmud that goes something like this: a lesson learned with humor is a lesson remembered. Let the joy begin and continue!

The purpose of this book and that of its two predecessors is to be a primer for the flower arranger, beginning or continuing education-minded, who is giving of her time and service to the decoration of her house of worship.

Much of the information here came from my own mistakes. My objective in all my years of arranging flowers has been to make new and more sophisticated mistakes, rather than repeat the old ones. It is my hope that you will use this little book to escape making my mistakes and move on to greater glory.

Confidence comes with repetition and experience. The more times you arrange even a simple bouquet for the kitchen table, the more proficient you will become, and the more you will enjoy the results. Experimentation and repetition are vitally important. They need not be carried out with expensive flowers from the florist: free material literally grows on trees, shrubs, stalks and bushes in your garden, your neighbor's garden and along roadsides (where legal, of course).

A touch of garden or field material actually adds to the uniqueness of an arrangement and avoids a professional florist look. These additions not only save money but also improve the end product. Flowering branches are especially wonderful. A trip to the grocery store will open many opportunities to use beautiful vegetables and fruits. Later, enjoy them at home or share them with the hospital or homebound. With a sharp eye and clever hand, costs can be kept way down and quality can be raised high, simply by keeping your eyes open to the beauties of nature. Your mind and your eyes are the only muscles you need to exercise.

Often, a neighbor's pruning pile on the curb waiting to be picked up is your treasure trove. Recycling is good, too. Ditches have reeds and stalks and the occasional flower. Utilizing a variety of materials and noting how long they last and how well they condition, will give you vital information on the durability and efficacy of plant material for future use. You can find branches and vines to fashion into a permanent wreath, which you can decorate for many occasions.

On the subject of cost, please note that churches are tax-exempt organizations. Use the state tax certificates to avoid paying sales taxes. Often stores will give a discount for not-for-profit organizations, and sometimes these tax numbers will allow you to purchase wholesale flowers and mechanics, which I will tell you about in Chapter 1.

Volunteer time and flowers are valuable also. This guide is intended to be user-friendly, budget-conscious for the church and environmentally kind. With a bit of foresight and opportunity, we can reuse, recycle, gather and adapt.

Having an understanding of design elements and familiarity with the plant material will greatly enhance your effectiveness, both in time and the final result. There are so many artful ways to create the illusion of riches: a few expensive, showy flowers, surrounded by lesser but appropriately chosen materials, can make a gorgeous showing. Small flowers may be bunched together to look like larger ones.

# INSPIRATIONS

# chapter and verse 1:
## A FIRM FOUNDATION – TOOLS AND MECHANICS

Tools are those items that are employed in the preparation of the plant material, and mechanics are those things that hold the arrangement together within (or sometimes without) the container. Surgeons cannot operate without proper instruments, and neither can we. Happily, all we need is readily available at garden, hobby and craft shops, home improvement centers, florist supply, florist shops, and hardware stores. Whatever you acquire, it is essential for your sanity and bliss to label it immediately and prominently with your name. Better yet, buy in funny, flashy colors to begin with. This way, you may only have to purchase them once. (This would be classified as a genuine miracle.)

Even in the safety of your own home, keep all tools together in one place, preferably hidden or labeled with a "do not disturb" sign in several languages with a skull and crossbones. The tools each have millions of other household uses, but it is best to have your own little cache. Acquire other clippers for gardening and duplicates of any other item you use for other purposes.

Always clean all tools after use with rubbing alcohol, bleach or one of those new biodegradable antiseptic cleaners. This will reduce the introduction of bacteria to your next stems. Remember, cleanliness is next to you-know-what, and this includes everything: plant material, tools, mechanics, containers and especially water. Ideally, when holding flowers either cut or in an arrangement, the water should be changed every day if you have that luxury. This will add days to your arrangement. You will change the water again and again, ad nauseum.

Clippers (not large pruning shears) are a must-have, and ratchet types are best for the stems. Most professional florists use a paring knife, something on the order of a Swiss Army Knife, but inexpensive ones may be bought at cookery stores or kitchen supply houses for only a dollar or so. Get the ones with bright-colored handles rather than foliage-green, as clippers and knives can easily get buried in discarded stems and foliage or hide under other things in the drawer.

Knife-wielding is both faster and better for the flower, but it takes practice. If attempting this, never move the knife: move the stem. A friend who teaches at the very special Mrs. Vietor's House at Pooh Corner preschool in Houston, Texas, told me they teach the Christopher Robins, who are five, to use this technique paring a carrot. If they can do it, we can do it, and it is better than learning

the hard way. I have the ouches to prove it.

Those beautiful Japanese Ikebana clippers are lethal to a person of my limited agility, as I pinch the fleshy part of my palm every time I try to use them. But they are highly recommended. I once cut myself during a lecture and was horrified to be bleeding in front of fifty garden club ladies. It was a Julia Child moment, for those of us old enough to have enjoyed watching the television cooking master drop food on the floor and slice and dice herself every now and then.

An Exacto knife can be used, but is rarely necessary and must be wielded even more carefully. Keep all of your cutting tools sharpened for better treatment of the plant material and your hand muscles.

A good watering can with a long spout can save you no end of trouble.

I marked mine with my name and bought it in an obnoxious orange color so I can always spot it; since they were on sale at the dollar store, I bought two!

## Bare Necessities:

Plant material, a cutting tool, some water, a watering can, a container and some time.

Mechanics can be anything from a rubber band or string to products available from the many sources listed in this book. They are simply the items used to stabilize arrangements to hold the flowers in place and assure the delivery of water to the plant material. Mechanics are like ladies' undergarments; they are meant to support and conceal, but not be seen. (Although some current Hollywood

fashion trends make me wonder if I should rephrase that statement: Let it show, or don't use any!) There are many ways to cover the mechanics, so what they are is not a large concern in the design process. A supply of extra filler or a handful of moss will do the trick at the end. The size and shape of the container and the type of plant material dictate the selection. Also, will the mechanics inside the container be returned after use? This impacts whether you use permanent or temporary mechanics.

In church arranging, remember that the viewers of your arrangement are on the other side of the altar rail and light is usually dim; they are also not seated as close as a table centerpiece. Therefore, the support can be covered by something as simple as the leaf or moss or you can even give the arrangement a modest turn to put its best face, and not its bald spot, forward.

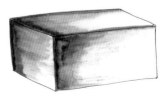

Floral foam, commonly called Oasis, is the most used mechanic. It comes standard in green blocks the size of paving bricks. It comes in five densities, depending on what you need: Standard, Standard Deluxe (for larger stems), Instant (which is great if you do not have the requisite amount of time to soak), Instant Deluxe (for thicker stems, fast) and Springtime (for delicate flowers with hollow stems). There are also different sizes for convenience: Designer, Grande, and Micro. Standard is just fine.

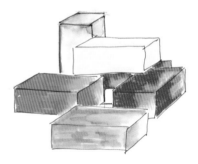

Within the last few years, Rainbow Foam, in the same block form, has been introduced, but it is meant to show and comes in a variety of colors. The latest version of this is a foam in powder form and bright colors. You simply add water. And when I say bright, we are talking seriously bright: orange, lime green, grape, yellow, etc. Since the colors are so blinding, I cannot readily think of a church application for Rainbow Foam, but it has potential for children's and spring activities. There is brown foam called Sahara (also known as Ultrafoam) for dried arrangements only. For heavier stems, there is Sahara II. Most florists I know simply use Styrofoam, which comes in white and light green.

Improperly soaked foam is one of the leading causes of flower droop. The foam acts by swelling around the stem, which gives the stem stability as well as moisture. Oasis, for fresh flowers, must be soaked in a pan of water, so that the block may intake water from the bottom: do not use the faucet or pour water over the top because at the center, where the stems are going to be, the block will remain bone-dry. The soaking takes two hours, and the block will become quite heavy. A standard block holds two quarts of water to be exact! Oasis likes to advertise, so when you wet your foam, place the writing side up and the little dots down.

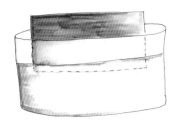

There is a type of foam called Instant Oasis which can intake water in less than one minute (45 seconds to be exact, according to the web site). Some types of foam come with chemicals to keep the flowers fresh; these must be soaked in the container in which they will be used; otherwise the chemicals will just be left behind in the soaking water.

There are other important floral foam caveats. The biggest causes of failure with floral foam are:

1.) Jabbing the stem in and taking it back out—this effectively plugs the stem so it is unable to drink. You have to place the stem carefully as you get only one chance.

2.) Using old foam. Foam has a shelf life and will begin to crumble and neither hold water nor support properly. That pre-owned Swiss cheese Oasis, as I call it—and you know what I am talking about: The one saved from an arrangement you received for your last baby or hip replacement—has had its day. Floral foam is not recyclable, except if you want to rewet it and stick sprigs of parsley or mint or other herbs from the garden in your kitchen to have on hand for one day only. It is actually very useful for this purpose.

If it is holey, it is not Holy. If it is pale and crumbly, don't even try. It costs very little to buy a nice fresh brick.

Besides the rectangular bricks, there are some other foam sizes and shapes available: Small and large round forms, semicircles, wreaths, crosses, hearts, and linking blocks for garlands, including a new, nine-foot garland. Some are fitted with waterproof backs for pews or altar rails in a variety of shapes. There are plastic holders that the Oasis fits into for hanging on pews, and there are little cages called Igloo holders, which come in several sizes. They are plastic holders for which you can buy fresh foam refills; some have glue on the back and can be stuck on things which look really cool.

There are also casket saddles from florist supply houses. They are plastic trays, with a waterproof base in which the foam blocks fit perfectly. They can be used for other things besides caskets.

If these goodies are not readily available at florists' suppliers, hit the Internet or read some of those loathsome catalogues that pour through your mailbox; afloral.com

and floralmart.com have great selections. Visit Smithers Oasis at www.floraloasis.com. It not only has a full range of items, but pictures of them as well. Be careful not to get the Canadian site; all the measurements are not in inches, and as I don't have a clue how big a centimeter is, I could get in real trouble there.

Oasis, may be shaped easily with a paring knife or a piece of wire, monofilament fishing line or dental floss.

Beveling the Oasis around the edges as well as shaping it to fit the container will remove the blocky shape of the brick and give you a rounded form instead of, well, a brick.

insertion will do. Plastic-wrapped blocks are available; if you use them, simply pierce the cover with the stem or a skewer. For tiny stems, use a toothpick or straight pin.

You can sculpt the foam also; wet your hands, take a knife and pare away like Michelangelo. If you need two or more blocks to fit together, take several wooden skewers (found at the grocers for kebabs and the like) and anchor the blocks together by placing the skewers at odd angles into the blocks.

You can use chicken or turkey wire to cover the foam for extra control. Just clip with wire cutters—not your precious clippers, please! Bend or adjust the wire over the desired shape of the foam and then secure it by twisting the loose wire ends together or by using anchor tape. Anchor tape is easily available at supply and craft stores. It is best used when you tape it to itself, rather than to the container. And if your foam is already wet, tape won't stick anywhere, no matter how hard you pray.

Remember never to jam any flowers in hard because the stems will get congested in the center; just a light

potato with plant material or moss so it won't show.

Don't put the foam at the same level as the top of the opening of the vase. Place the foam above the lip of the container so you are not stuffing flowers inside. Instead, form a little collar of foam at the top (just about the size of a clerical collar or two). Don't let the foam come over the edge horizontally of the lip, as it will leak water.

Here is arguably the weirdest mechanic of all: You can stick stems into a small potato. No watering, no mess and woody stems handled this way will stay fresh a long time. Simply slit an insertion point into the potato with a knife and insert the stem. The moisture and starch in the potato does the trick. This technique is especially useful for stems of ivy. Put some foil or plastic wrap under the potato to protect in the unlikely case of spoilage. Then simply conceal the

After foam, the next most used mechanic is the aforementioned chicken or turkey wire. Thankfully, you don't have to go to the feed store to purchase a huge roll, as it is available in small amounts—at triple the price, of course. You can cut the wire just as you would to cover the Oasis, but this time you ball it and fit it into the container. This works better in tall vases than low ones, as you can imagine. Inserting the flowers in the holes gives you control and stability. The added advantage is that you do not have to cover the wire or wait for it to soak. A warning about containers: Use an inner liner as the wire obviously scratches the inside of the vase. Even plastic wrap will help protect the inside.

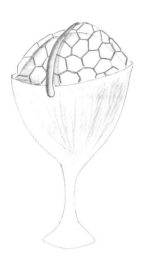

When you use chicken wire, you still want it to come up over the lip of the container, or you will get a squashed look as if the flowers were trying to escape out the top. Once you have built your cage, it can stay in the container for the next time as long as everything is clean.

You can also twine soft branches around each other, which looks quite decorative in a clear container. This natural armature will require water changes until your branches have become completely dry but will keep its shape once dried.

Another method of designing I like is to hand-tie a bouquet and then simply place it in the container.

Lay out the flowers on a table and pick up one stem at a time with one hand and place the stem in the other hand. Alternate the plant material and twist the bouquet slightly in your palm. You will be amazed at how many stems you can hold in your hand. The only tricky part is tying it. With your free hand, tie the bouquet with raffia, string or twine (use your teeth to help in the absence of a third hand). Then trim the ends of the stems at the bottom, and place them in the container. This method keeps the flowers snug, and they don't move around. I prefer hand-tying to floral foam any day, and it is very economical. It does take a little practice, however.

Thinking about mechanics reminds me of an amusing story: A volunteer at my church had a flower that was going to be way too tall for the arrangement. A co-worker suggested to her that she cut it. The horrified designer cried, "But that will ruin it." The other lady replied with a great deal of patience; "I mean from the bottom, not the top!" Remember, just because you have it, you don't have to use it!

Permanent mechanics are the rocks of ages. The simplest forms of permanent mechanics are rocks and pebbles. Rocks or shells can be collected or scooped up from the driveway; however, the cleanliness rules apply. They are a bother to wash properly, and I would use germicidal soap. I have jammed my kitchen garbage disposal several times; little rocks in the gears can be a big expense. I now wash down gravel outside with a garden hose until the runoff is clean.

You can buy clean gravel or rocks used for aquariums from a pet store. I like to fill all my containers with pebbles for ballast and extra hold; the amount depends on the depth of the container. Clean sand is okay, but it can clog small stems. Pretty shaped and colored rocks can be found at craft shops and upscale places like

Smith and Hawken, and again are very decorative in clear containers. You can pick a color that is compatible with a stained-glass window, the season or the flowers you are using in the arrangement. Clear crystal and clear rocks pick up candlelight and rays of sun beautifully, especially through stained glass.

Manufactured mechanics are commonly called frogs, and they come in a variety of shapes and sizes. There are the cage type, the pin holder type and various other combinations and permutations. They are heavy and somewhat expensive but can be used over and over again. They can be very user-friendly and deliver more water to the plant than the floral foam.

Flower cages allow for a free-flowing arrangement. They are heavy and stable, but they sometimes need to be supplemented by florist clay

applied around the bottom for a firm hold. Since the clay is hard to remove, using an inner liner is a better choice than sticking mechanics in the bottom of your beautiful container. Museum Putty and Museum Gel are amazing products. They hold tightly and then are removable. I would give them a try; they might be difficult to find, but they have many uses. They are used by museums to hold down valuable vases and urns on pedestals, so you know they are secure.

Pinholder types hold the stems rigidly in an upright position. They are perfect for stylized designs in the oriental manner, but not always the best choice for a design requiring a large number of stems. Here is a tip for pinholders: paring woody stems helps not only to make them fit better but also allows room for more stems. And an old stocking, cut and pressed over the needles of the pinholder

base, helps keep it free of old stems and foam. You just remove the patch of nylon and replace when necessary.

Why pay for long stems when they are covered up in the vase? If you wish to use a deep vase, fill up the container with clean gravel and place the cage or pinholder on the top surface of the gravel.

Keep it in the container permanently. Sometimes, the gravel will be sufficient to stabilize the arrangement. Marbles are not efficient as they were meant to roll around heaven and earth all day, and they do. They are a nightmare to me, although I imagine the marbles are having a wonderful time.

A caveat on all permanent mechanics: they are expensive, so use them only when you have a prayer of retrieval. Since they are in the bottom of the container, they might be overlooked and tossed out or passed along. If, by any miracle, you are able to purchase a cage with a pin-holder in the bottom, snap it up, love and cherish it. Mark it with your name.

A kensan is basically a pinholder in a self-contained unit. It is fabulous for small arrangements for the obvious reason that it holds a small amount of water. Kensans can be obtained in black, green and metallic, or you may paint them any color you wish. You can make your own kensan by taking a clean tuna fish (or such) can and permanently gluing in a pinholder. A glue gun—I prefer the safer, cooler wax guns—or any waterproof adhesive will work (even the dreaded floral stickum, of which I am not a

fan). A good source for kensans and other useful mechanics is www.stonelantern-highlands.com.

Another option is the orchid tube or aquapic: A tube which you fill with water and insert a stem through a plastic cap. These pics are useful for short stems placed higher up in the design and for individual stems inserted into wreaths and swags. Some of these pics come with a pointed end for sticking into foam or the soil of a potted plant.

You can use pot plants and combine them with cut flowers in pics, producing what is called a pot-et-fleur. The rooted greenery, ivy is superb, can stay for the duration, while the cut flowers can be changed out as needed. This technique is good for any holiday from Easter to

Christmas when the decorations must last. You can plant the ivy in the churchyard later in some climates, and use it for cuttings when you need those trailing vines or some filler.

You can also fashion a very effective and simple device known as a kubari out of a branch of a tree or shrub.

Another useful item is a wreath ring. These have many uses for holiday designs, not just Christmas. They make a beautiful Advent wreath, especially if two are lashed together with paddle wire to make a thick and full wreath. Which brings us to paddle wire… Read on.

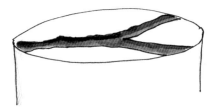

Find a small branch with a crotch or "Y" shape and whittle it down carefully to fit very tightly into the mouth of your container. This gives you a permanent tripartite section in which to create loose arrangements with a bit of control. Wet the branch for each use. It will shrink a bit when dry and will fall into the container between uses, but have faith and do not discard it. In fact, the bottom of the container is an excellent storage spot for your kubari.

# chapteR anÒ veRse 2:
## THE TIES THAT BIND – CONNECTIONS

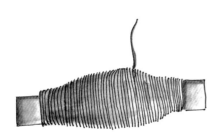

Paddle wire is so useful you will wonder how you got along without it. It fastens everything. The little paddles come in gauges from very thin (30) to thick (20). The 22, 24, and 26 gauges are multi-purpose, strong and flexible. The wire can be used for cutting floral foam. It is much more efficient and quicker than using a knife. One caveat, do not take one of these little paddles in your carry-on luggage at an airport, as the X-ray people are very interested in a bunch of coiled wires.

You can buy small packets of straight-cut wires which are even handier, but more expensive. Sometimes you can also find annealed wires which are covered in a fabric of light green. These are neat because they do not scratch pews or other furniture. But, unfortunately, they are hard to find. Chenille sticks (pipe cleaners, essentially) are somewhat obtrusive but do come in all colors for blending in from a distance. Twist ties, available everywhere, are dandy for tying.

A small length of wire will support a floppy flower head or a wobbly stem; if you insert it up from the bottom of the stem, it does not show. For the top of a floppy head, such as a gerbera, insert the wire through the top of the flower, and snip any remaining wire from the top. As a last resort, wind the wire on the outside of the flower stem.

Bind wire is a new product from Oasis that may be cut and reused. It comes in natural and green. It is flexible for tying but will not give support. Raffia is a natural material and is unobtrusive and/or decorative in casual situations. When you use raffia, wet it first, and when it dries, it will bind even tighter. And, believe it or not, even Scotch Tape can make an effective mechanic; just criss-cross it across the top of the container in a grid.

Since the wire obviously shows, use only when the stem can be concealed among the other flowers. Florists often use this technique to support their flowers as it is fast and easy.

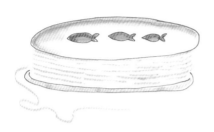

All God's children need monofilament wire or fishing line. This comes by the pound weight it can carry. A roll of ten-pound test weight is probably as strong as you need; and the all-but-invisible line can attach or hold bunches of plant material together where another method might show. It looks like dental floss and will not harm furniture when applied properly. Most houses within 100 miles of a boat or a body of water probably have this line in a drawer already. If you can't find it at home, it is available at hardware, fishing, and sports shops.

Because the wire is nearly invisible and tedious to tie, it helps to tie your knot over a dark colored surface so you can see what you are doing. Also, unrelated to flower arranging, remember that this very handy wire will cut cheesecake better than a

knife. And all this talk of fishing line reminds me that a tackle box is particularly good for keeping your flower supplies together.

Collecting a full working kit of flower-arranging tools can take you from one end of the mall to the other. You will hit craft, sporting, and hardware stores, cookery shops, and other unique emporia before you run out of places to find useful equipment.

But, back to binding. There are many adhesives on the market. 3M has a spray product called Super 77; if you prefer a non-spray product, there are several brands in tubes; an effective one is by, you guessed it, Oasis. You can literally glue a petal or a leaf on with this adhesive. Floral adhesive may be used to anchor a mechanic or inner liner into a container as a safety net, but I find it gooey and hard to remove. It is sold in rolls like ribbon, and you strip back the two waxed sides to expose the amount you need. If you choose to use it, apply on a dry surface only. It comes in both white and green.

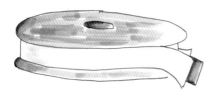

Anchor tape, which comes in clear and green, is a stronger version of Scotch Tape. Use liberally to wrap wire to foam or foam to the container.

Fern or greening pins are hairpins for plant material. You can use them to fasten one thing to another or to place moss around an arrangement. The pins have many other uses in arranging and can keep an unruly flower or leaf in place.

Floral picks from W.J. Cowee are small green stakes which come in a variety of lengths with a point on one end, both with a copper wire or without. The pointy end can go directly in floral foam or a piece of fruit. The tie end can be used to fasten sprigs or berry branches together for sticking into the arrangement. More inexpensively, you can purchase wooden skewers at the grocery store to use as pics. Then later, you can eat the fruit you used. An improvement on the straight pic is a folding one; these are known as Dumas Picks. They can be hard to find, but they are worth the search.

# chapter and verse 3:
## FROM WHENCE COMETH OUR HELP – RANDOM AIDS

Handy helpers include plastic drop cloths, butcher's paper, long-handled watering can, kitchen baster and syringe, at least two deep buckets, old washcloths and inner liners (so the inside of the vases do not get scratched).

Plastic drop cloths are fabulous because you can just drop your stems on the floor and pick up the whole mess to carry to the trash after the arranging. The drop cloth saves the floors and pews as well. Paint stores carry them, and most likely dollar stores do too. If you tape them to the floor, they are less prone to slip around.

Butcher's paper is waxy and water-proof, a perfect cover for work tables or altars. These rolls are available at

Sam's Club, Costco, and the other wholesale and retail places of your choice, as well as kitchen supply stores. Secure the paper with painter's masking tape—the kind with the distinctive blue color. Water rolls off and nothing gets stained. Butcher's paper can become slippery if used underfoot, so sensible shoes are a good idea, but aren't they always?

Other things worth having are a long-handled watering can, a kitchen baster and even a syringe, available from the pharmacy, for adding water

in tight places. Deep buckets to hold fresh water and plant materials are a high priority. If you do not wish to purchase them from the florist supplier, you can recycle buckets from condiment containers from restaurants, private clubs and such. After you have cleaned the India relish remains or mustard out, stack them carefully as they fit snugly. Four can become one again, and it is a tug-of-war to get them back apart.

Drying and clearing leftover foliage out of your buckets is a must after each use, as bacteria will grow and damage the next flowers placed in the bucket. Take them outside and hose them down. You can use chlorine bleach (just a tablespoon or so for a large bucket), antibacterial soaps, or products bought at the florists for this purpose.

Important tip: Put your name on your buckets too, along with a strong admonition not to discard.

Another indispensable helper is an old washcloth, which is a handy foliage remover. Hold the stem in one hand, and with the other, wipe the cloth down the stem to pull the leaves off. The cloth will protect your hand and the foliage comes off easily. For obvious reasons, this method will not work—for either you or the flower—on roses, because of the thorns and bruising of the stems. Since rose strippers are too rough, these beauties should be gently defoliated by hand.

And I cannot say it often enough: It is a good idea to use inner liners in any opaque container. These can be purchased from a floral supply house or improvised from recycled plastic containers like cottage cheese, yogurt, etc.

Cone-shaped vessels, which florists use for cemetery arrangements, often fit well into the church containers. They come from Panacea Company and can be found at craft stores. They have a removable spike and cost about one dollar. The spike may be placed in sand, rocks or the soil of a potted plant to stabilize the liner. They are useful with and without the spike.

Check with the florist who does the most weddings/funerals at your church and find out what they use for inner liners and see if you can purchase some. Some churches have custom-made metal containers from a local tinsmith. It takes vigilance to keep them from walking away to hospitals and shut-ins or being sent back to the florist by mistake. Any florists who work regularly at your church will be ecstatic if you have them available.

A good purchase is a large, inexpensive composition container— the kind florists use when you cannot see the container. They are made of a sort of waterproof papier-mâché.

Here is an odd useless fact you can share with your volunteers next time you use a composition container: papier-mâché just means chewed-up paper in French.

I learned a good way to anchor huge mass arrangements in a container with an inner liner from Jim Johnson, director of the Texas A&M University Benz School of Design. He uses a hog ring and applicator, and these act as large staples. They are found in feed stores, not widely available in our large metropolitan cities, but, to my surprise, easily available at Amazon.com.

Hog rings are fast and awesomely stable. To add to the hilarity, they come in sizes: pig, shoat and hog. (I believe hog to be the largest). They have many applications; they hold on plant tags and all sorts of things around the garden. You will wonder how you ever got along without them. Total cost is only about eight dollars for the rings and applicator.

You have to go to an agricultural school or read my book to learn these things. I cannot tell you how much of the information in this book I have obtained from attending Mr. Johnson's classes, which are conducted on the A&M campus. If you have the chance, they are wonderful, low-key and fabulous. All levels of expertise are represented. You can find the schedules on the website, aggie-horticulture.tamu.edu/benz.

Also pertaining to agriculture, a tomato cage can become a large cone-shaped mechanic as well. It is great, as it is already the shape of a Christmas tree; just stuff it with Oasis or chicken wire or moss.

INSPIRATIONS

# INSPIRATIONS

# cHapteR aNÒ veRse 4:

## OUR CUPS DO NOT RUNNETH OVER – CONTAINERS

More than anything else, the container will dictate or suggest the amount and type of plant material to use as well as the type of mechanic required to secure your beautiful creations. And once again: cleanliness is next to..., so the container needs to be pristine inside and out. If the container is leaky or very valuable, an inner liner must be used. There I go again with the inner liner. Even a baggie can be used with a rubber band to hold the water. Paraffin can be applied to leaky containers for a seal. I have heard, but not tried, that cracked ceramic containers can be made waterproof by placing milk in the container and letting it sit. I assume you place the container in a larger milk-proof container to do this. Let me know if it works! If you have used all of your cottage cheese containers, there are wonderful inner liners at very reasonable prices. They come in both plastic and papier-mâché in green and white, but ReCreations has some in basil, natural bark and fieldstone—in other words green, brown, and off-white. These liners are good-looking enough to show.

As I mentioned under Mechanics, you can bring up the bottom of a deep container with clean rocks and save money by purchasing shorter stems. A clear plastic product called Lexan, bought by the sheet in plastic supply places, can be cut to fit underneath the container, insuring protection for the surface on which the container is used, should a leak occur.

It is important to stick the tip of your finger in the top of the container to feel if the arrangement needs more water or is about to overflow. It is always important to check after moving an arrangement, and to top it off with clean water when it is in its final "resting place."

The shape of the container will also dictate to some degree the final size and the shape of the arrangement. A tall container will direct plant material into a tall arrangement; a shorter one leaves latitude but will most likely be a shorter finished product.

The usual height ratio between plant material and container is that the plant material is one-and-one-half times the height plus the width of the container. This is pleasing to the eye; however, it is no longer a hard-and-fast rule. The numbers have to do with the divine proportion or golden mean, and this is so complicated I am not even going to try to explain it to you. There is a fine book by Dan Harwell, *Searching for Design*, listed in the bibliography, concerning this intriguing phenomenon, if you are interested. It is called phi, actually pronounced "fee." If you drop this

information in a conversation, you will really impress people!

I once was lecturing to a garden club many years ago and carefully explained and demonstrated the one-and-a-half-height rule. The rule applies to width rather than to height if the predominant shape of the container is horizontal.

They were having a flower show later that month, and when I returned to the city to judge it, the entries chairman, who was also from out of town, asked me, "What on earth did you teach these ladies?" It turned out that one of the entrants thought I meant to measure from the floor and not the bottom of the container on the table; she had a very tall container with less than an inch of plant material! She told the entries chairman that is what I told her to do. Oh, my!

Episcopalians, Catholics and Lutherans, among others, are kneeling people, so be sure that there are sufficient downwardly placed stems to give a finished look from below. For that matter, a whole bunch of flowers should be inserted up into the arrangement from below. Kneel to see how it looks when you finish, and make sure it is good from that angle.

When working with pairs of altar containers, the general shape of the arrangement must be the same; and if the arrangements are not triangular or round shapes, then you need to decide if the direction will lead up to or away from the altar in the center. (See illustration, I cannot possibly explain this.)

Two teams were working in my church one rushed holiday season, and we did not notice that each of them was banking flowers with the low end to the right and the high end to the left. We were all so busy trying to get out of the way of the prayer service and get to our own Christmas preparations that we failed to notice this until we stepped back into the nave to admire our work. From there, it looked as if when the choir arrived, they should burst forth with "Nearer, My God, to Thee" as the effect was that the church was listing on one side and the icy Atlantic was just out of the porthole. One team had to graciously start over. It was not the greatest moment on that December day, but better than being on the actual Titanic!

Pairs do not need to be identical; divide the available plant material equally into two buckets and use the same material in each. It works well and is far more interesting. You really can't match exactly anyhow.

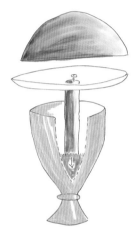

The size of the mouth or opening of a container may restrict the amount of plant material you can use, especially if you're using branches and large stems. You can simply cover the container lip with a clear dish or pie plate on a dowel and place sand or pebbles down in the vase to anchor the plate, which will rest on the top of the container. You may either tape or glue this down. Lomey company makes dishes for this purpose; they may be found at florist supply places. You then add your floral foam, also anchored in the plate or vase and you can have a wonderfully full arrangement and use much shorter stems. This can even work on a candlestick.

Beautiful clear-glass containers are wonderful too, and jewel colors can really add a lot, especially on festive days and events. You can recycle clear containers into colored splendor to complement the stained-glass windows by purchasing colored, transparent spray at craft shops and applying it yourself. Pebeo is one of the best brands, but make sure it is transparent as it also comes in opaque. It is available in spray as well as jars for use with a brush, but using the spray and applying it as directed gives a more uniform color.

One of the most wonderful containers is the Baptismal Font, but not everybody approves. This is definitely a check-with-the-rector "situation." In the UK, they do it in great style, and it is a natural. The bowl can be resplendent. I was able to arrange in the baptismal font only once when we had a new dean. It was a congregation-pleaser, but not so with the staff of our clergy. Once again, an inner liner is mandatory. That's enough about that. I then began garlanding the font (as illustrated) and then doing private decorations for private baptisms, where the family of the "baptisee" donated the money for the plant material. Since there was no set price, I just made do with what the donation allowed. I always put some plant material or flowers from my garden as my little gift to the baby. I made a tiny bouquet at the base so that the family could have a small memento of the occasion. It was almost as much fun as putting flowers in the basin.

To swag the font, I would sprint up to the choir where the font was located, just after the eight o'clock service, and wrap the garland and get out just before the nine o'clock group came in. When I could get down to the floor and back up again, I could often be found by early attendees sprawled on my tummy with my shoes off, fussing with the final flounce. In order to do this rapidly, we carefully measured a section of cording to encircle the font and attached it with a device called a swivel or bolt snap on one end and a steel ring on the other. They are easily available at hardware stores for pennies (well, dimes anyway). It is the same principle as clasping a necklace.

We tucked soft branches, asparagus fern, leaves and flowers into the cording; they could be out of water for the duration of the two services to come and easily and quickly dismantled.

Don't forget baskets and terracotta pots for use as containers. Craft stores have wonderful spray and brush paint in a number of colors, including metallics made by Patio; it is very durable and the colors are most agreeable. They will work well on both basket and pot! Krylon puts out a satin-metallic finish, Plasticote brand has a textured finish; there are antiquing kits for faux patinas. There are even washable paints called Clean Colors, which children can use as a Sunday school project.

If you wish to cover terracotta pots with moss: first clean the pot, then brush glue all over the outside surface. (Elmer's and Aleene's are good brands). Using disposable gloves, apply the moss, which may be bought by the case. It can be used for

various occasions, and I will tell you more about it in Chapter 6.

A recent innovation, available in florist supply places, and everywhere soon I suspect, are small battery-powered lights. If they are not in water, they will last for a week, and if submerged in water, they will last for three days. They come in different colors and have obvious uses where wax candles do not work. They can be attached to swags or wreaths as they come with a cord for hanging. They also come in short votive-candle style with a battery which can be turned on and off. There are colors for any season and occasion. They really add a lot where corded lights cannot be used or candles are not feasible. The company that makes them is called Acolyte.

Another wonderful new and improved product is double-sided decorative ribbon. I recently saw an ad for it at Jamaligarden.com in New York, and they ship. (And they have divine, reasonably priced containers.) There is such a science to bow-tying, and the double-sided ribbon takes most of the challenge out of it, even for all-thumbs me. When it comes to tying bows, no child of mine would ever let me touch her sashes—how they knew how terrible they looked from behind is still a mystery to me, but I guess they could see their sister's droopy, off-centered sash and deduced what their own must look like. In any case, they would run screaming for anyone nearby to tie their sashes, even strange women.

Since then, I have learned that the most important activity in tying a ribbon is tightly holding the center with your finger—or even better, the finger of a friend. This is another case of needing three hands. I have tied my finger into the bow many times, and it can hurt. This is another reason I adore wire-edged ribbons, which you can just get your more adept guild members to tie into bows. After you use them, you simply hang them on coat hangers and put them in a plastic bag. Take them out next year, fluff them up, and they are ready to go again. You can add the ends, or tails, later. You just tie off a length of matching ribbon in the middle, sparing some wire to add to the center of your bow, and voila! Twin tails! They are best clipped at an angle, not a blunt cut. Fold the tail in half and cut across it at an angle. This gives a

nice V shape. Another idea, which is nice with some ribbons, is to tie a little knot in the tail about two inches above the ends. This is very chic.

# chapter and verse 5:
## BESIDE STILL WATERS – WATER AND CONDITIONING

Only a few cut flowers and foliages can remain fresh without being in water. Think of a fish out of water. Even if stems do not flop around, think of what they are feeling! Try to keep the stems in the water during the entire process and get them back in as quickly as you can. Whether you have gathered material from your own garden or from the florist, place in clean water as soon as possible and make a fresh slanted cut on the stem end. Make a new cut each time you have to remove them from the water.

Proper conditioning enables the plant to take up more water, making it viable for a longer period of time.

Cutting underwater for the last cut is especially beneficial, as air does not have time to get into the stem. When you move the stem to the arrangement from the cutting water, there is enough moisture on the cut end, due to surface tension, to keep the seal. Change the cutting water often to keep it fresh and bacteria-free. (Bacteria clogs the stem, and it cannot take up water.) Not to change the subject, but I cannot say this often enough: Change the water in the holding bucket every day if you possibly can.

Here is a quiz: When you go to the grocery store and buy peanut butter, orange juice, and triple-fudge-brownie-deluxe ice cream, which do you put away first? If you said peanut butter, you should not be allowed to handle floral clippers at all. Obviously, it is the ice cream, then orange juice, and lastly the peanut butter. It is just the same with flowers. When you return from the florist or from picking your flowers in the garden, place the most expensive and most fragile flowers in water first and work down the chain until you get to the foliage filler.

Roses and lilies are usually going to be your most delicate and expensive flowers, so start with them. Remove all foliage which would go beneath the waterline, and pick off any foliage you do not need; this assists the flower in not having to compete with the foliage for water and will increase its life. Eliminating the unnecessary material under the water also retards bacterial growth. Swamps have their value for teeming life, but they are

also very smelly (and a lot of that teeming life is bacteria and up to no good). Adding a splash of soft drink with sugar such as Sprite or 7Up will act as an antiseptic. (I have no idea why, but the carbonation is beneficial.) This solution also feeds the flowers. However, the use of raw sugar will harm the plants by clogging them and will draw unwanted drinkers to your bucket. A good solution to use to condition your flowers is $1/2$ water, $1/2$ regular Sprite, and 1 tablespoon Clorox bleach.

Some scientists at Massachusetts Institute of Technology were experimenting with products to condition flowers. As a joke, they placed a stem in one of their Cokes in the lab. They discovered the number one—the absolute number one—best way to preserve the length of a flower's life was Coca-Cola.

On a large scale, Coke is not cost-effective, so this information is not really relevant and no help whatsoever to the florist industry which commissioned the study. The jury is out on a penny in water—which will close your open tulips, or keep closed ones from opening—but an aspirin does make sense, as does adding a piece of willow, from which aspirin is made. There are commercial products on the market which do the same as the soft drink, i.e., provide food and a bacterial retardant; but use sparingly, as at full strength they can cause the flowers to mature faster and not last. A shot of adult spirits does very nicely too, but the flowers take up the scent of the alcohol.

One year, I thought an orange scent would be nice in my Christmas tree water, so I added Cointreau to the water. The Cointreau smell was horrible in the mornings (better in the evenings) as the house smelled like a margarita. The tree was large, so this is not a big worry in a small arrangement. Do remember that gin will definitely give off a juniper scent, and vodka is the most neutral. Sprite is a lot cheaper, but do use the real thing as your flowers do not need to be on a diet and do not react to artificial sweeteners.

On the subject of water additives, I mentioned before that bleach is a good thing to add to your conditioning water. It helps fight bacteria, but use only a tiny bit as it could bleach your flowers, and the arrangement will also smell like the cleaning closet.

There are some plants I like to use that are naturally smelly; for instance, the cruciferous family: Ornamental kales, cabbages and the like. To neutralize their odor, put a dab of rubbing alcohol on a cotton ball and place on the end of the stem; then wrap each stem and ball in Saran wrap and use a rubber band, raffia or string to hold the ball on, and place the whole package into the flower arrangement.

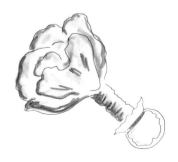

Misting with water is helpful in keeping a fresh look. Even easier is utilizing one of several products on the market, which act to keep the flowers from losing moisture. One is named Crowning Glory, another Final Touch, but there are others. They can be used on all cut materials. Think of them as hair spray for flowers. You need to spray only once when you have finished arranging. Transparent flowers, such as poinsettias and orchids, will spot if misted with water or the anti-desiccants, so do read the label, as boring as that is.

Some exceptions to the water-needy plant materials are certain reeds and grasses, succulents, mother-in-law's tongue (we know how strong those are), bromeliads, protea, and tropicals in general. Tropicals (heliconias, gingers, anthurium, etc.) do not intake water from the stem, so misting them is sufficient. In Hawaii, they condition the tropicals by putting them upside down in buckets. Heathers and ericas are wispy and textural but not thirsty. See the glossary for plant materials for long-lasting arrangements as well as delicate ones.

It is best to keep everything in water except desert-dwelling plants and wildflowers. Gray and hairy foliage will turn green with too much water, as it doesn't like much moisture. It is helpful to remember the plant's natural environment. Desert plants don't get much in the way of water, tropicals don't have much soil and need to drink by rain, but regular flowers, on the other hand, like a good drink to thrive. The longer the plant's growing season, the heartier it is likely to be and the longer it will last in your arrangement.

## maintaining temperature

Tepid water will help refresh plant material when you are beginning preparation. Misting the arrangement and making a tent of a plastic laundry or garbage bag will preserve the finished arrangement for later use. Florists use this method as they must hold arrangements overnight or even several days.

You can force flowers to open with a deep-warm-water bath. Replace the warm water every twenty minutes for three sessions. I have used a hair dryer set on low to open buds about ready to pop (take care not to cook them). The hairdryer is great for amaryllis.

Conversely, you can retard the opening of older or rapidly aging flowers by placing them in cool water in the coolest location possible. The deeper the water, the better they condition. There is always the refrigerator, too.

One year, our garden club hosted THE Annual Meeting of our organization, and we wanted to use all roses from our gardens from Beaumont and Houston. We picked them all carefully in the cool of the morning or evening, and warmed, chilled, or closeted them if necessary. Then we refrigerated them for several days until we had enough, each at the peak of perfection. With more than fifty tables thus adorned, the room was amazing.

But even with perfection, taste does vary. There were two members from separate clubs who were in charge of assembly and placement of the arrangements in the ballroom. One went along putting baby's breath in all of them, and one followed her, pulling it all out. In, out, the pattern repeated up until the last minute. Neither was wrong, so remember to trust your taste in your arrangements, and they will look just fine. Choices will always remain a subjective matter. Just so you know, the no-baby's breath won the contest. Flower ladies are flower ladies.

Arrangements will drink the most in the first hour; they can be bone-dry in two hours if the flowers are thirsty. If using floral foam, dig a small hole in the foam in the very back of the arrangement, so that you can add water. Again, there is no substitute for the finger test. You want to top off the tank without overflowing on the fair linen. The finger test avoids spills and mop-ups. I have done both.

In a nutshell, here is what you need to remember about conditioning:

- Gather materials first thing in the morning or late in the evening when moisture is high, so that the shock is not as severe to the flower.
- Let the fresh-cut stems harden in water overnight. Ideally, water the garden area thoroughly an hour or two before picking.
- Condition the most expensive and fragile flowers first, of course. Place and keep them in water as quickly as possible.

# chapter and verse 6:
## CONSIDER THE LILIES – FRESH FLOWERS

Part of our obligation to this wonderful Earth is not to use plants that are scarce and/or endangered. It is just as important not to encourage viewers to use flowers that are invasive. And after you consider the moral aspects of certain plants, some just work better than others.

For information about caring for individual flowers, I found a great source at plantanswers@tamu.edu. Some flowers need special care and attention. While almost all flowers need water, some have oozy latex in their stems, and they will clog the other flowers' stems and cause them to wilt. Daffodils and other members of the narcissus family, for example, are notorious, so keep them out of the general water bucket and in their own separate one. Be suspicious of any oozy stem and keep it separate.

Some reliable materials I like to use are ruscus and lemon leaves (salal), aspidistra, leather fern, privet, hosta, boxwood, liatris and liriope (lily grass). Alstromeria is wonderful to use if you can get the picture out of your mind of it sitting in the soy sauce glass container in Chinese restaurants. With some very good hybridizing, the colors are quite lovely. Some people are allergic to the leaves, however, so they are best stripped away. All of these are very reasonable to purchase. Steel grass, wonderful galax leaves and cordyline (ti) as well as a lot of the palms are also long-lived. Yes, even gladiolus, commodores and carnations, which always remind me of funerals, are very long-lasting.

Horsetail reeds and bamboos are segmented and hold water in each section, so they can be used as mini water holders throughout the arrangement. Just poke a wire or sharp instrument down the shoot to the depth you want.

While tropicals are easy and reliable to use, hydrangea, lilac, Queen Anne's lace, wild carrot, spring bulbs and flowers with a short-bloom life are a challenge to keep fresh. In fact, all umbel shapes are fragile as they are made up of many tiny flower heads which are naturally delicate. Try dragging the stems of these flowers through alum to change their PH. Stock, gladiolas, carnations, baby's breath, alstromeria, bells of Ireland

and all chrysanthemums are reliable and reasonable in cost.

I used to positively cringe at the thought of it, but what they have done in recent years with baby's breath and gladiolas has made me change my mind about them. The industry has experimented with amazing sizes and colors, and I am quite happy to use either of them. Taste, like choice, is an individual thing unless it is by committee, and then, heaven help us.

Remember, the use of garden flowers, branches and foliage gives a distinctive and natural look and avoids that sent-to-everybody's-mother-on-Mother's Day look from the magazine and TV ads. I'm not saying that they are bad, they're just generic. No, they are bad.

With the jet age and heavy production in the Southern Hemisphere where the seasons are reversed, it is simple to get almost any flower we want now. Some things do remain seasonal and, of course, prices vary on rarity of season. When purchasing, buy the freshest plant material you can find. Check the bottom of a bunch of flowers to see how the stems look. Avoid mushy stems and yellowing foliage and stems. The south end should look as fresh as the north end of a standing-up bunch of material. If you just have to have a particular bunch of tired flowers, then bargain. Ask your salesperson when the flowers came into the shop. Yesterday or this morning is good; around February last year is not.

Sometimes the flowers have just arrived and have not had time to recover; they are fine if you have the time to let them drink. It is smart to ask the florist when their normal shipments come in; in large cities flowers come in often, but in smaller areas they don't arrive every day. Wash up after arranging with flowers from other countries; their laws on pesticide are not as stringent as ours, and some of the material, especially roses, have been heavily treated. There is an organic rose farm in Ecuador: www.inguezaroses.com. They are gorgeous and very fresh.

It was once considered de rigueur to smash stems, but it is only necessary for extremely hard, woody stems. The idea is to let more water in by breaking up the surface, but if one takes out one's aggression on the stem

and smashes it to bits, it will not be in any shape to take up water. Cut the bottom in the shape of a cross (easy to remember) and slit or pare some of the bark away from the base.

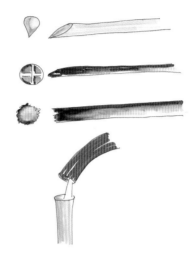

Hollow-stemmed flowers benefit from being filled with water. Turn them upside down and fill them from the faucet or a watering can. Hold them shut with your thumb, and place them directly into the foam. Really large stems like amaryllis can be stuffed with cotton or taped shut with water inside.

Ferns, greens and most foliages love an overnight bath. Toss them in a tub of water with a newspaper on top to hold them under, completely submerged. I recently learned maidenhair fern benefited from having the stems dipped in some salt.

Fresh new growth can look fine, but might not be mature enough to last in an arrangement. Vines and nandina (heavenly bamboo) can wilt and cause great disappointment by service time.

The addition of fruits and vegetables in the arrangements is a dramatic and economical touch. They can be impaled on pics, skewers or wires and possibly recycled. But remember, roses and apples are not a good combination: Roses are very susceptible to the ethane gas emitted by apples which causes them to wilt rapidly.

Speaking of roses puts me in mind of including scented flowers and foliage in our arrangements. Rosemary smells wonderful and lilies are heavenly; even carnations have a bit of scent. Other good-smelling plants I like to use are real lemons and limes, hyacinths, lavenders, fir trees, freesias, gardenias, scented geraniums, pittosporum blooms, jasmine, muscari, mock orange, spirea, trachelium, verbena, and some azaleas. With so many to choose

from, it would be a shame not to have your arrangement smell as nice as it looks. If an arrangement with these fragrant plants is placed near a candelabrum, the candle warmth brings the fragrances out.

There is another source of plant material known as roadafolia; i.e., plants growing along ditches. Covet plant is that which is growing in your neighbor's garden. The first is yours for the adventure, and the second may take some charm and persuasion before liberating.

All flowers continue to open after cutting, so be wary of lilies. They are simply wonderful, but as they open, the stamens appear. The stains from those stamens are murder to remove from those white vestments and any clothes you might be wearing. Clip out the stamens as soon as they open. This can be a long process, as they open rather suddenly and in sequence, not all at once. I guess you could keep a pair of small scissors in your handbag for those between-the-services touch-ups. If staining does occur, applying Scotch Tape or masking tape works sometimes, and Oxyclean and similar products are very effective for wine stains, lipstick from the communion cloth and pollen. My daughter, Adrienne, thinks Oxyclean is so strong it removed her fingerprints, but I still have mine, so don't worry.

If you are making a crown of thorns, flying dragon or green dragon citrus have fierce thorns. You can cut them and soak them overnight to soften and make them more flexible, then weave the crown and glue or tie in a circle. It will dry and can be used many years.

Mosses are available in several varieties, all with slightly different uses for covering holes and any mechanics that might be showing. Sheet moss is the most common and comes with a little turf, which is thin but in irregular shapes as they harvest it in little clumps. It is good for gluing onto objects (permanently) and stuffing into arrangements to hide mechanics or fill spaces. Mood moss (green moss) is very decorative and comes in much fatter, rounder clumps and has a much fresher green color. You can use this as the top dressing or base of potted plants; it lacks pliability, but can be glued onto a round dry Oasis to make a beautiful topiary form.

There is also Spanish moss, which is actually a bromeliad, growing on trees

in the South and available elsewhere.

If you pick your own, do put it in the microwave accompanied by a cup of water to remove the inhabitants. I learned the hard way that they can emerge at the most embarrassing time during dinner parties and crawl toward the guests. Use gloves in working with moss as a precaution of picking up a rash or infection if you have sensitive skin. Moss is messy to work with, so use a good floor cloth and a well-ventilated area.

A less attractive option to me, as I am not a fan of Astroturf, is to purchase a moss carpet. It started out as real moss, but after being cleaned and sprayed a green color, it was backed with mesh. OK from a distance, and you can cut it in any shape. It will probably never fade.

Green up real live moss by putting a bit of moisture in a plastic bag and refrigerate. It will perk right back up.

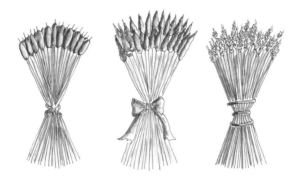

# chapter and verse 7:

## GLEANING THE FIELDS – DRIED FLOWERS

Late summer, fall and winter offer great opportunities for finding dried materials, so no season is without opportunity. Look for them while walking the dog, or looking for the cat, or while on vacation.

Preserving plant material in glycerin makes beautiful dried material. To make the solution, place two parts hot water to one part of glycerin. After stripping off an inch or two of bark on the end, put the stem in solution. You will need to add more solution as it is drawn up slowly by the plant material. It usually takes about two weeks. If the foliage is large such as Ti (cordyline, pronounced tea) or aspidistra leaves, you will have to keep swabbing the material with a cotton ball. As glycerin is expensive,

ask for technical grade rather than laboratory grade. It is available in any pharmacy. Some leaves hold their colors as if fresh; others change dramatically; have fun.

You can also dry material by hanging it upside down. A dark, dry location will preserve color best. This works for herbs, cockscomb, maidenhair fern and dock, among others. Dock, like cattails, may be spritzed with hair spray or any fixative to prevent, or at least retard, the bursting of seed heads or whatever they are. Baby's breath, hydrangea, mature seed pods, pine cones and statice dry naturally and look more or less the same as when fresh. Blue and yellow flowers especially retain their color.

A microwave will do a beautiful job drying rose petals; put each individually on a plate and make sure they do not touch. You will have to experiment how long is long enough, but start with a very short time. They can be scattered as a decoration or used to make potpourri from a wedding bouquet as a keepsake.

There are kits for serious flower drying and preserving, but my climate is too humid for much success. You can place items in silica or kitty litter and try to dry them. It is advisable to put the kitty litter where the cat cannot get confused.

By accident—some of the very best training I have ever had—I left some bells of Ireland in a container of water and forgot about them. Gradual desiccation made a gorgeous, but fragile, bunch of angel skin-coral stems. They couldn't take much handling, but they were breathtaking. Just letting arrangements gradually lose water can produce some interesting dried material.

Pine cones and seed pods, such as eucalyptus, look the same dead or alive. Experiment and be surprised. You can also spray the results for added strength; matte, not glossy, finish is more natural. There are wonderful fall berries and fresh,

beautiful fall foliage at our disposal as well. It is really the fall colors that count; mums, bronze flowers, deep crimsons, dark yellows and oranges work well for the season. Use the fresh and dried together. You can take vines, supple branches and reeds and bend them to your liking and tie them in rubber bands and give them a good overnight soaking. Let them dry naturally, and they will retain memory (maintaining their tied shape) when dried. They are wonderful for a long time, just not forever.

And remember, if these drying techniques are too time-consuming, or end unsuccessfully, dried flowers can be bought from growers, garden shops and at fairs. Knud Nielsen has quality dried material and will send a catalogue; check them on the Internet.

In addition to dried flowers, when you cannot water due to the container or location, there is another option. I, being a garden enthusiast, am not partial to fake flowers, which the floral trade calls everlastings, but some silk flowers are absolutely gorgeous. And, of course, they will last as long as needed with the occasional good dusting. In the long run, they are by far the most economical. The further away you place them from viewers, though, the better!

Good quality permanent garlands and wreaths are available at craft stores and go on sale just after the season with phenomenal savings, which is fantastic for a small budget. They still take skill to arrange and place and can be mixed with fresh material and bows; the only downside is storage.

# chapter and verse 8:

## ACTS – DESIGN

Even though flower arrangements are usually flowing and free and can look amorphous, they are essentially geometric forms: triangles, rounds, pyramids or obelisks, and fans (upside-down triangles).

### mass & Line arrangements

Mass arrangements have a closed form, and line arrangements an open profile (voids or non-material become part of the design). There are of course line/mass and mass/line arrangements, which are a bit of both. A mass arrangement simply has more solid forms than voids (air), and line arrangements feature a visible line as the main design element.

Shapes are either symmetrical, where each side of the arrangement would have roughly the same visual weight and material as the other if you drew an imaginary line down the center, or asymmetrical in which the arrangements are not equally centered. If you are working on a pair of arrangements—as we so often do—be sure they are the same general shape.

## pLant materiaLs

The three types of plant materials in arranging are line, focal and filler.

Line materials are thin and tall: strap leaves, lily grass, gladiolas, stock, aspidistra, liatris, reeds and grasses, flax, branches, etc., are examples. These form the outline of your arrangement.

Focal material is usually large and round and important such as roses,

lilies, hydrangea, daisies, carnations, tulips, sunflowers, etc. These are usually the expensive flowers that you should condition first and give the most care. As the name implies, they are the point of interest or focus.

Filler is comprised of lesser flowers and foliage: boxwood, small flowers such as genistra (broom), goldenrod, baby's breath and heathers, etc. These are the least important things and are added last, as the name implies, to fill out an arrangement and to hide the mechanics and any unwanted "holes." The filler needs to be chosen carefully to complement the rest of the material.

Begin establishing your outline by placing your line material to form the boundaries. Place material at the tallest and widest points in the arrangement, being careful to place the stems at different angles to avoid a flat look. Use different angles for all of the subsequent placements too. You are working in three dimensions.

Next, place your large round focal materials low in the arrangement, slightly over the lip of the container to visually anchor the arrangement. If the focal flower(s) just rests on the rim and does not come over the sides of the container, it will completely divide the container and the plant material into two entities which will not be very friendly with each other. It will appear they are trying to avoid one another, and the eye will stop at the unintended line formed between them.

Just as you do on the Christmas tree, use smaller forms higher and larger forms lower. Remember that gathering a bunch of smaller flowers and forming them into a bunch can look the same visually as a very large flower head. If the large forms are placed too high, there will be nothing to anchor the arrangement, and you are guaranteed to run out of material. This is a rookie mistake that need never happen, but I have seen this time and time again.

Here's another rookie error that you can avoid: Just because you have it, does not mean you have to use it.

We now know that cleaning your plate is not the very best thing to do, so use what you need and avoid sticking something in just because you have it. The exception is Aunt Ruina's rose which she just picked for you to use, and you know she will be sitting in the front pew looking for it. By all means, put that rose front and center.

I once did an arrangement demonstration in Natchez, Mississippi, to the venerable ladies of the Pilgrimage Garden Club. They had clipped for days and everyone had brought flowers; they had assembled containers for me to arrange in and there were at least forty. I began toiling through all the material and containers and reached the end of the lecture time and then some. The chairman stood up and proclaimed, "Shall we keep on going? Lunch can wait!" There was general approval of this idea, and I soldiered on. I was besieged on all sides with "use this branch from Meg's garden" or "why don't you use Aunt Addie's roses," or "Mrs. Chace's fine silver bowl would look beautiful with flowers in it."

For the finale I created an enormous mass arrangement with everything under the sun in it as two people handed me flowers. There were also enough centerpieces for all the luncheon tables and a few in the windowsill too. Whew. But, back on subject:

After you have sketched your parameters with your line material and anchored your design with the focal point, you are just painting by numbers. Work all over the design and all of the way around, adding the filler material; if you just work in the front, you may have the arrangement fall forward with weight. It will also look flat.

You do not have to put the best material in the back, but it is necessary to have it fully filled to look rich, complete and three-dimensional. You can use stems, stalks, and extraneous broken flowers but do fill it three-quarters of the way around.

Lastly, cover the mechanics with filler, moss, galax or leaves. The eye should move throughout the arrangement and not stop on a "bull's eye," one dominant element which causes a pause in the eye motion. There is the "Lone Ranger" rule, too: never use just one of anything.

Also, there is another look to avoid: two flowers placed at the same height give an unwelcome effect I call the "Mickey Mouse." If you create two ears, the viewer's eye will ping-pong between the two of them.

One other colorful phrase: Be sure to leave space for the butterflies to fly through. This admonition is likely to be nearly as old as the Bible itself.

Floral Arrangement Checklist once you feel you are done:

- Check for visual and real balance.
- Trim, but do not pull out any placed material; snip it out to avoid disaster. I have seen it all fall apart; I have done this, but only once.
- Check the water. Is the arrangement thirsty?
- Is it placed far enough away from candles, drafts and vestments?
- Tell yourself how good you are.
- Check the arrangement later to see what has opened up, moved toward the light, wilted or shifted. Consider the lily stamens.

- Check water again.
- Replace, as necessary, with your extra material which you, of course, always have.
- Tell yourself again how good you are.
- Tell someone else how good she is if she has assisted you. Go ahead, make her day.

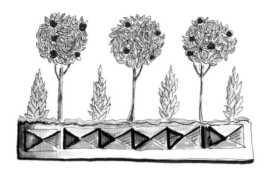

# cHapteR anð veRse 9:

## THE GOSPEL TRUTH – ELEMENTS AND PRINCIPLES OF DESIGN

There are attributes or fundamentals that apply to any composition. Design is made up of elements each dependent on the other. Often it is hard to tell where one ends and the next one begins, as they are so interrelated.

### ðesigN eLements

The elements of design are: space, size, form, line, color, light, texture and pattern.

Space: The space within which you have to work, your imaginary boundaries based on the placement. You want a large form to fill the space if it is large, but you never want to overfill or crowd. Nothing should touch the imaginary boundaries.

Size: Physical volume or space taken up by the arrangement. Imagine a cube and set your arrangement within that space.

Form: The shape, solid. (Usually a geometric form).

Line: The bones or structure of the design formed by the linear elements (spiky stems, branches or flowers).

Color: Very simple and very complicated! It is how the eye perceives light rays. The characteristics are hue, value and intensity. Color has both a physical and an emotional impact. The warm colors—red, orange and yellow—appear to come forward, toward the viewer; the cool colors— green, blue and violet—recede and fade to the background. The warm colors energize; the cool colors soothe. The time of day the arrangement will be viewed makes a difference in the selection of color, as the soft cools will fade in the evening. This is important for weddings, as the blues and violets do not show up under artificial light. On the other hand, warm colors can be distracting. White stands out beautifully under all light conditions. Yellow, which can be read as gold, is equally arresting. Monochromatic arrangements, those using tones, tints and shades of one color, are always effective. In that vein, all-green arrangements are quite effective and can be quite handsome without flowers. Remember interesting choices such as bells of Ireland, grocery vegetables—which are fantastic green accents and focal points—and ever-handy houseplant foliage. Bamboo is ubiquitous and very useful. There are thousands of shades of green.

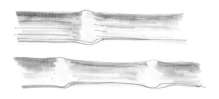

For maximum impact, more color material and less foliage filler will result in a more luminous arrangement. Everyone over four years old knows the primary colors red, yellow and blue. Combined with each other, they become the secondary colors: red+yellow=orange; red+blue=violet and yellow+blue makes green. This is the most elementary color wheel. When used together exclusively, the primary colors set each other off so that the effect can be startling, strong, modern and not particularly pleasing. Complementary colors are made up of a primary and the secondary that is opposite it on the color wheel. When used together, they tend to highlight each other and intensify the color. Complements are red and green, yellow and violet, and blue and orange. If you go a bit further, you get the split complements which break down the colors even more, and you add a third set of options.

Red-orange, yellow-green and blue-violet form split complements on the color wheel; and split complements are optimum for harmony. Look for foliage with a blue or gray cast, or rust-colored foliages and flowers to enhance the arrangement or container. A popular color combination right now is dark purple (blue violet) with chartreuse (yellow green) and pumpkin (yellow orange). The cool tones and the warm ones interact in a wonderful way. Live a little and experiment! There are very few true colors—note the warm or cool undertones. Mixing them is not pleasing to the eye. Stay cool, or get warm. Train your eye!

Background is another consideration once you determine the design, color and materials. Keep in mind, dark leaves will not show up against a dark wall. Carpets, windows, seasonal hangings and other features of the church as well as the seasonal hangings will be a factor in your color choices. A red arrangement is beautiful with a red carpet.

Light: How much light will there be, and where is the source? Is it natural (sunlight) or artificial? Is it day or night? Detail will show more in bright light.

Texture: The visual and actual feel of the materials. Simply, it is the rough or smooth quality in flowers and foliage. Texture can convey

mood, i.e., prickly thorns for the Passion, smooth lilies for serene occasions. It is necessary to have contrast in textures.

Pattern: The various elements visualized as lights and darks, shiny and smooth, etc., within the whole. Squint at the arrangement to determine pattern. Everything has pattern: shadows, fabrics, etc.

## ᴅesɪɢɴ ᴘʀɪɴᴄɪᴘʟes

The principles of design are balance, proportion, scale, rhythm, dominance and contrast.

Balance: Visual and physical stability. It must not only have the weight distributed properly, but the eye must perceive the arrangement as "comfortable."

Proportion: Comparative size of the components. Remember, in traditional arrangements the overall height is one and one-half times the height or width of the container. Equal visual amounts of plant material and container are to be avoided: it is boring to the viewer as there is not a dominant feature.

A very large magnolia leaf or hosta placed with baby's breath will accentuate the size of the large one in contrast to the size of the smaller one. The charm of this arrangement is that they are not related to each other except as parts of the plant kingdom. Some may think this is too far a stretch, others may want to be adventurous.

Scale: Includes both the appropriate size to setting and the appropriate size of the plant material to the other components.

Rhythm: Just as the notes in music create a melody, repetition in the florals you select establish the harmony of the design. This refers to the speed and path which the eyes move through an arrangement. The eye usually follows from one focal point to the next. The idea is to move the eye around and not stop it with a Bull's Eye. Instead, use at least two stopping focal points, and three is better.

Dominance: There must be one dominant and at least one subordinate element, or the composition will look bland.

Contrast: Light and dark, small and large, smooth and rough, all are contrast just like night and day.

We design something every day

when we coordinate what we wear; jewelry and makeup, if applicable, or a tie with a shirt, if applicable. (Real men arrange, too.) The process is what Mr. Johnson calls "making a clear decision." You address just one decision at a time, based on the objective of creating a beautifully coordinated design. The process is much more mental than physical. (Although everyone who has conditioned a bunch of flowers knows how much physical effort is put into the preparation.) Take one question at a time, and then move from there—always keeping your objective in mind. With a clear focus, your decisions will be much easier. Think of the process as being like a pilot's checklist, or *Flower Arranging for Dummies* (if there is not one already. I'd love to write it).

Just keep looking at beautiful arrangements and develop the "eye." Keep track of why you think it is beautiful. This is an exercise much easier than obtaining rock-hard abs! Exercise eye and mind. Then repeat.

Here is a basic checklist for you:

- Which container are you using?
- Where is the arrangement to be placed and for what purpose?

Size
Color choices
Shape
Formality

- How long need it last?
  Plant selection
- How much room do you have?
  Limits
- If you must bring the arrangement from home, is it stable and will it fit in your car?
  Mechanics
  If this sounds dumb, I once made an arrangement for a flower show, only to realize it was too tall for the car. I took it apart to transport it and, believe me, it did not win a prize! If wedding flowers are to be moved to the reception, factor the move into your design choices too.
- Will the design be viewed from all sides or just the front?
  Placement, amount and distribution of plant material
- At what time of day or night will it be viewed?
- What are the light conditions and sources?
  Color choices
- What is your budget?
- Which mechanics best suit the container and the material?
  Maximum hold or a loose bouquet
- What plant material goes best with the container and the setting to address the occasion, budget and time frame?
  Formality and conformance to the container
- From what height will it be viewed?
- How much time do you have and how many helpers?

Factor all of these in one at a time, and you will have your decisions narrowed to easy steps.

Once you have your arrangement completed, remember to leave room for the movement of the clergy, and avoid placement near candles. Make sure that there is space between the wall and reredos (the facing of decorative screen behind the altar) or the retable (the raised shelf sometimes found behind the altar). These assume a freestanding altar. Many rectors do not wish the flowers or branches to come up above the cross, so do check.

# chapter and verse 10:

## GLORY BE – SPECIAL DECORATIONS & SPECIAL OCCASIONS

### the cross

As I mentioned, some priests do not want the flowers to go over the top of the cross, so always check before you design. I was so frustrated by how low our cross was at Christ Church Cathedral in Houston that I talked the clergy into commissioning a small base placed on top of the tabernacle on which our cross sat. It gave us more height on either side of the cross. Every florist in Houston loved me as it gave them more leeway for better proportion.

So think about placing a platform for the cross if you have a short one to contend with.

I also like to place a small, low container at the base of the cross, use vines to twine around the arms and tuck tubed flowers behind the cross arms.

can be painted any color to match the altar. The flowers will completely cover the Oasis; even though it is random, the effect is a true expression of the joy of the season. You can also cover a plain wooden cross in chicken wire and stuff it with moss into which the flowers are inserted. There are both dry and wet floral cruciforms available for smaller congregations, Sunday school classrooms or youth groups to flower.

## fLOwering the easter cross

A delightful event at Eastertide is the flowering of the cross when children and/or parishioners bring flowers to place on a special cross. A permanent cross can be constructed by a carpenter and used each year. The frame should be the width of Oasis blocks, so that they slip in one on top of the other in the arms and down the length of the cross. The foam should be fairly dry but some waterproofing will still be necessary in the base, since you will need enough water in your Oasis to anchor the cross. Flowers can be placed across the base, a tin liner filled with water. The wooden cross

## paLm sunday crosses

Palm Sunday crosses are fashioned from fronds of last year's palms. Take one end of the frond, loop it halfway down towards the back, and then draw it out and across to make the arms of the cross. Fold over the back and glue.

## maypoLes

Maypoles have their roots in a slightly shocking pagan ritual celebrating fertility, but it became a community and parish competition in the 1600s in the UK to have the prettiest Maypole. Bright ribbons are affixed to the top of the pole, and children, usually girls, take the free ends of the ribbon and dance around it in an in-and-out pattern—some from the left and some from the right. The dance results in an interesting pattern of colored ribbons wrapped around the pole. It is a spring celebration, often celebrated at Eastertide.

## fLooR vases aNÒ taLL caNÒLesticks

Floor vases need tall arrangements proportional to their height. These vases are often tall and spindly with a small mouth that can be a problem. To maximize the volume of plant material, use the mouth of the vase only as a platform. Ignore the dimensions of the narrow mouth, and affix a saucer to the rim using floral adhesive. You can glue or nail a dowel to the bottom of the saucer, and anchor it in sand for stability.

A glue gun will make the nail hole waterproof. Select the mechanics necessary to hold your arrangement firmly. Once you make it, it can be used over and over.

If the vase is really tall, a tomato cage (found in garden stores) or hanging-basket cage can be attached to the saucer and stuffed with foam. Another method of gaining height is to place a small dowel in the vase and impale Oasis blocks upon it. This technique will allow you to use very short stems which are always more economical.

You can also use potted plants taken out of their pots and placed in plastic bags. First, water the plant thoroughly. Submerge the pot in water until moist throughout; drain away any excess water.

Then, place the root ball in a baggie and zip or tie to seal in the moisture. When your bags are all filled, wire one on top of the other, and anchor the whole package inside the cage.

Use greenery to hide the bags and cage. Poinsettias do not like excessive moisture; do not oversoak the soil.

The plants will remain fresh, even lying on their sides. Ivy is spectacular, and even poinsettias work surprisingly well treated this way. The soil mix that the plant came in will tell you how wet the plant "wants" to be. If it is in a very porous soil, mix with lots of vermiculite particles (those little white dots): be careful not to over-soak; it can get too wet and rot from the roots. If the potting medium is heavy, the plant needs lots of moisture. Mist flowers or foliage as needed by observation. You should not have to open the sealed bags. Do not mist poinsettias as they will spot, and do not use anti-dessicant spray on live plants.

## oTHeR CoNTaiNeRs

Using baskets or decoratively painted pots can also make a very effective decoration in the church. Patio paint is very durable and comes in many colors, including metallic. This is a way to hide the terracotta or dark green plastic color. Spraying will make a smoother finish, but remove plants before spraying. I probably didn't really need to say that, but after some of the things I have seen and done, you never know.

Remember, if you use a glue gun or good floral adhesive, you can place moss over the entire surface of the pot. For a garden look, spray soapy water on a pot. While it is still wet, spray it with green paint. When it dries, soap it again. Use more paint in another shade of green. This is fun to do, and it looks mossy.

## hedgerows

Hedgerows are small "gardens" placed on the floor. You can use plastic liners from garden shops and nursery supply stores or loaf pans from home. They are basically window boxes placed end-to-end. You may plant the containers with de-potted material (with root balls) or place

prepared Oasis and/or chicken wire in each container and arrange fresh-cut flowers in them. When they are filled, line them up end-to-end. Save some filler to join the ends, and you have a nice hedge of material to line the front of the choir stall or the altar rail.

Many volunteers may participate in creating their own private gardens and then just join them. Here, as in paired arrangements, an equal proportioning of flowers will produce the all-in-one effect. Establish a height, and then just arrange away; you don't need to worry about a focal point or a side or back filling as they just snug up to something. If they are to be viewed from both sides, then of course the back needs to look as good as the front. This is a great activity for children too. There is no wrong approach, and the result looks terrific.

## carpeting

Carpeting is a paved (or pavé) technique using short flower blossoms in shallow pans, to form a floor tapestry. The pans are placed close together to form a pattern. Fill the pans (cookie sheets with sides) with either wet or dry (for dried arrangements) floral foam. On each, place a pattern drawn on brown craft paper or transparent tissue. Etch the design right into the foam. Cut the stems very short; if the stems are weak, use a toothpick to make the hole and secure the flower with a straight pin. Set the flowers in very closely so that no foam shows. Mist with water to keep them fresh, although the short stems assure plenty of water to the flower head. One of the anti-desiccants will improve their durability. Carpeting can be spectacular placed down the center of an aisle, but they are very time-consuming unless you have lots of volunteers. This is a universal truth.

## garlands and swags

Christmas greens come already roped and, considering the preciousness of time during the season, it is well worth the extra money. The professional product is better-looking, too. However, innovations have improved greatly the ease of making swags. There are foam-filled cages which can be linked and filled. These just require stuffing with material which hides the plastic cages.

Fresh foam refills are available. Also, you can string your own garlands by taking two long leaders or wire, and, starting with one bough, twist the tie on another bough about halfway down. Keep going and twist each on to the other. Keep the boughs all going in one direction or, if you are framing, have them meet in the middle.

Garlands must be misted to be kept fresh. Use floral anti-desiccant and fireproof spray if you are using them near candles or if city or county ordinance requires it. It is never a bad idea, anyway. Fruits such as lemons, apples, oranges, lady apples and kumquats make a nice addition for a "Della Robbia" look.

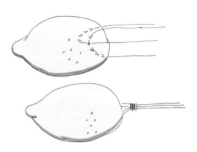

Impale the fruits with a pic with wire or use heavy 30-gauge wire for more flexibility and strength. Use two wires so you can twist them together. Push one wire through the stem end, and bend it into a U shape inside the fruit, do the same with the second and you will have two wires to twist together, leaving enough wire to secure the fruit on the wreath. You can cluster several bunches of berries with wire for more impact. Berries stay on the branch longer with the foliage removed.

You can also make your own swag by using sleeves of plastic in which you put wet foam. Sleeves may be made out of plastic trash bags or plastic newspaper covers. Slip the wet foam in and tie very securely and string them end-to-end like linked sausages. Stick the stems through the plastic. This is somewhat messy and time-consuming but cost-effective.

Dried or everlasting swags are fine, and some fire codes demand them; you can make them more attractive with the addition of fresh flowers or fruits. I am not above giving a light spray of gold or silver paint to some of the finished swag to give it a little liveliness; Design Master makes a floral spray. A little goes a long way; just apply an occasional light dusting. This is so not-garden-club, but it is effective.

## BOWS

Bow tying is simple for most people besides myself. With the new double-sided and wired ribbon, there will always be at least one of your volunteers who can tie a beautiful bow, even if you can't.

## WREATHS

Wire frames can be found at any craft store. If you are starting from scratch, just add a snippet of material at a time in a straightforward fashion around the ring, tying and bending sprigs to the frame with pics, binding or paddle wire. Other items of interest can be added after you have finished.

A mixture of greens is more interesting than using all of the same. There are Oasis and Sahara forms in all sizes. To be fun and different, try a triangular or square wreath; you can make the frame yourself. And here's a cautionary note: Bought holly is harvested well in advance of the season and does not hold up. Pick your own whenever possible.

Cut the ribbon to desired length and simply lay the ribbon on a table and fold back and forth, twisting it as you reach the center. In that direct center of the stack, use wire to tie together; fluff out the loops you have created. You may add "tails" by incorporating them with another wire at the center. Make the bow appear more dimensional by making your first layer the longest and then gradually shorten the following folds. The first layer will determine the size of your bow.

## weddings

There are so many books on wedding flowers, my head spins. All of the fundamental things discussed will apply, with the additional factoring of the bride's or the bride's mother's, stepmother's or mother-in-law's— whichever one of these ladies who is really running the show—choice of color for the bridesmaids' gowns. In my day, the bride wore white, but today black is apparently the new white. The budget, any additional honorarium to the church for your labors, and the portability of the flowers should all be factored in. All of the elements should coordinate with the central color and the formality of the wedding. Also check the yellow pages for rentals on arches and such.

There are bouquet holders available at florist supply places that make the bouquets a snap. Remember to watch out for flowers that stain—the priest might forgive you for getting lily pollen on his vestment, but do you think the bride will? Boutonnières for the gentlemen—if they are not in bowling attire—are simple matters of rolling the flowers in floratape stem tape and pinning with boutonnière

pins with the fat heads which come in pearl and black finish.

Corsages for the mothers and house party are a nice touch; they now are usually worn on the handbag instead of on the shoulder, as there is less area to pin them on all those strapless dresses. There are flower "purses"— little waterproof silk bags—for sale. Lomey company sells one with ruffled edges and plastic bouquet holders in a number of styles. One company calls their bouquet holders "wedding belles." Saints preserve us. The Stemson Company even makes floral stems which you can just jam the flowers into and save the wrapping for the corsages. I am not making this up. Dakota Plastics makes pew clips that come in brown to match wooden pews, but you could spray-paint them for different effects. You just fill them with Oasis and add your flowers. What will they think of next?

## memorials

Flower wreaths and stands are often donated by people wishing to pay tribute to the departed; however, the permanent vases still need attending. Usually, casket flowers are best done by a professional, but many times, friends donate flowers to be used on the casket or in the vases in churches where this is allowed. Flowers from friends are a lovely touch. If you wish to do them, there are several inexpensive plastic casket saddles available at florist supply stores. There are small green plastic vases from a company called Panacea Garden with spikes to go into the ground for tributes at the burial site. These containers have other useful applications as inner liners. The colors and choices of the flowers should reflect the individual's personality and the family's specific wishes.

## ofrendas

There is a charming custom celebrated in Mexico and by extension here in the Southwest. In the weeks before All Saints Day, November 1, and All Souls Day, November 2, altars are set up to celebrate the Day of the Dead beginning with October 31, Halloween—the Eve of All Hallows. Ofrendas are a nice idea for youth groups and children. The tradition consists of making an altar, usually a table with candles, filled with gifts or offerings to honor a beloved person who has died. Ofrendas are respectful remembrances of the departed, and the altar honors them by showing reminders of them or their favorite objects. The table soon becomes full of delightful toys, flowers, and other small items such as shells or postcards. It is a celebration of a life and a way of communication. A delightful quote from Carlos Loarca says, "The remembrance of the living creates the life of the dead."

I have seen delightful ofrendas in Mexico and Texas with tequila bottles, plates of beans, rosaries, dressed skeleton figures, fruits, dolls, candies and cookies, and the sugar skulls which are sold near the cemeteries. They are eclectic, to say the least, but they are a nice touch of remembrance, as well as an expression of the joy of having known that person in the past.

Red cockscomb and marigolds are the traditional flowers of the Day of the Dead, but many plastic ones appear joyfully on ofrendas. They are prominently placed in the doorways in Mexico for all to admire and share in the experience. Some communities have contests for best-decorated.

These celebrations can be a wonderful seasonal tradition in our churches, and another way to use flowers to communicate emotion.

# chapter and verse 11:

## A SEASON FOR ALL THINGS – A TIME TO SOW & A TIME TO REAP

### seasonal opportunities

Thanksgiving, a uniquely American holiday, brings a special service in which we acknowledge our bounty and express gratitude.

Loaves, sheaves of grain, gourds and pumpkins, fall foliage and berried branches are appropriate. As I mentioned earlier, berries may be tied by the bunch with monofilament or wire to other branches, or added to existing bunches to make them appear fuller. Grapevines hold up very well without water if you give them a drink the night before. Submerge them in the bathtub for best results.

If you use fruits and vegetables, it is better to not cut them, as they can be messy. Use caution, so it doesn't look like a buffet on the altar. Fall flowers tend to be the rich golds, reds and deep purples of the season. Dock, a roadside dweller, is a great line element and has wonderful texture. Turned foliage is delightful and plentiful. Cornstalks are another source of plant material. Those wonderful Chinese lanterns are very showy.

Wheat sheaves are beautiful for Thanksgiving, and actual loaves of bread may be treated with polyurethane or Thompson's Water Seal and used for many years.

I went to a bakery and bought the most wonderful selection of shapes and colors of unsliced breads: braids, rounds, and oval loaves. They looked so very biblical. For cleanliness and to render them reusable for the next year, I sprayed them with lacquer for the Thanksgiving altar the evening before. After turning them often, I left them outside to dry overnight. The next morning the raccoons had gnawed through each and every one, and dragged them up the entire length of the drive. Obviously they didn't mind the taste, and apparently they suffered no harm as they were back into the trash cans the next day. It is still advisable to spray in the open air,

but maybe early in the morning, so you can bring them in before the night creatures stir.

Winter and Christmas are times of evergreens, symbolic of everlasting hope and the return of spring. Keep them fresh the whole season by misting and coating with Crowning Glory, Wiltpruf, Final Touch or any other anti-desiccant. Greens will be fresher if you harvest your own; but be mindful you are pruning the tree which might affect its shape in the spring. Pines, firs and cedars are better suited for indoor use compared to spruces and broad-leafed plants. Ivy and magnolia work well. Rosemary is evergreen in the south and has a nice scent when you touch it or place it near candles. Fruits such as citrus and apples last longer than flowers.

Red poinsettias last better than the pink or white and are traditional Christmas flowers. However, there are some lovely new cultivars, some bi-color with a marbled or speckled effect. There are creamy white, pink, yellow and peach varieties. They have no symbolic significance, they just bloom in December in Mexico and are forced in many greenhouses for the season trade. They do not need much water and should not be misted. They do well with the bagging procedure around the root ball. They hate changes in temperature and drafts.

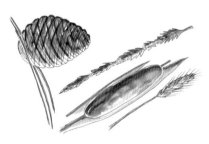

Even bare branches can add texture and interesting lines to an arrangement.

Pine cones and pods can be sprayed with clear lacquer to shine and reflect light. And I never mind a bit of gold dusting from commercial flower coloring sprays to add a discreet bit of shine, as I mentioned earlier.

Spring is the time of renewal. It has the most abundance of the bulb flowers of bright fresh colors, but they have a short life span. Because of their relative fragility, they need to be handled carefully and always kept in water. Bright pastels of the season and the delicate scents are best for this time.

Happily, there are some really wonderful palms for Palm Sunday available, and one does not have to use commodore, which looks like either a funeral or a chain store decoration, in my opinion.

Easter lilies and calla lilies are particularly delicate.

They are long-lasting and have a rich appearance because they have such substance and opacity, but bruise easily. Careful handling and deep watering will make these precious flowers last. Trustworthy statice and stock can be used as filler. While tempting because of their beauty, hydrangeas and lilacs can wilt in a second. Lilies of the valley might as well be gilded for what they cost—at least here in the South—but they grow in the ground in New England! Carnations, chrysanthemums and other staples can fill around a few lilies as focal points. Sometimes buying and cutting potted lilies is feasible, but they must be clipped the night before

arranging and allowed to harden in deep water. In the South, you can replant the bulbs.

Summer yields weeds (just a plant without a pedigree, according to the late Lady Bird Johnson), daisies, reeds, herbs and vividly colored flowers. They are easy to condition as the field flowers are used to dry, hot conditions. All green arrangements go well with the green hangings of Pentecost and are cool-looking against the heat.

## symbolism

The Victorians loved to give flowers symbolic meanings, and some are rooted in antiquity.

Lilies are symbolic of purity. The word chalice or vessel relates etymologically to the calyx of the lily, and the Virgin Mary. Lilies also have the trumpet shape suggesting the announcement of the Annunciation. They are the quintessential flower for Easter.

Orange blossoms are also associated with the Virgin Mary and signify happiness and fruitfulness, and are therefore associated with weddings.

Lilies of the valley and rose of

sharon (also called althea) are mentioned in the Bible in the Song of Solomon, referring to a love that— like the love of God—endures.

Anemones are a sad reminder, as they are supposed to have sprung on the ground beneath the Cross of Jesus' Crucifixion. They may in fact be the lilies of the field. Red poppies have long been associated with veterans of war and are very appropriate on Memorial Day.

Carnations represent pure love, and they are very appropriate on Mother's Day as they have begun to take on the symbolism of that day, as well. The legend says that carnations sprung up from the tears of the Virgin Mary after the Crucifixion.

Thorny plants recall the crown of thorns.

Roses have a great deal of symbolism associated with the Virgin Mary—the rose with no thorns.

Oranges and lemons are also associated with Mary, often pictured with the tree beside her, and the orange fruit in the hand of the infant Christ.

Pomegranates, an age-old symbol of righteousness which even adorned the Temple in Jerusalem, suggest eternity and are often found decorating vestments and religious artifacts. They are beautiful to use on altars, uncut. Cut they are beautiful, but disastrous for staining.

Grapes and wheat sheaves signify the Eucharist. Dogwood blossoms, because of their cruciform shape, are often considered symbolic, and the trefoil shape of the clover suggests the Trinity.

The palms used on Palm Sunday reflect not only the people laying them down in front of Jesus, but also the symbolism of triumph and praise. Laurel is victory, cedar consecration and cypress mourning. While there is weeping cypress, these associations with mourning actually go back to a beautiful ancient Roman legend about Cyparissus, who cared for Apollo's pet deer. There was a tragedy, which I won't go into here, and the custom arose of burying cypress branches with the dead.

The holly and the ivy, immortalized in the old carol, suggest the combined characteristics of the holly—its thorns, its blood-red berries and its pure white flowers—and the ivy—symbolic of holding the crown of thorns.

All flowers, especially spring bulbs, are a symbol of death and resurrection; they start out buried in the ground, and then in the spring they burst forth in glory.

## Recycling

A surprising amount of the time, a florist does not wish to come back to take away the flowers used at a Friday or Saturday night party. The party-giver usually does not want to come back the next day, either. All during Christmas one year, I pulled up to our club early in the morning and took away (with permission) the beautiful and very expensive roses and other lovelies. The altar decor looked different each Sunday, and the lucky brides were treated to some very nice flowers since they were not allowed to change the Christmas decor. I simply clipped out the old and stuck in the new at the church. I would pull up with my buckets, pluck the flowers out of the arrangements and place them as needed on the font or on the swags on the choir stalls. The church got free flowers, labor is saved by the florist (of course, you are the labor), and the clubs and halls are happy to begin setting up for their next event and save labor costs as well.

Many flowers, such as hydrangea, baby's breath, and statice look just about the same dried as fresh. You can use them again and again. Recycle everything you can, and often you can use it more than once. What is set out for the trash pickup on the curb may be another source of treasure; a neglected vine on a fence on an empty lot may be just what you need, and you helped some landlord with a needed cleanup. "Keep out" signs should be honored, especially here in Texas, where a lot of people own guns!

INSPIRATIONS

# chapter and verse 12:

## HALLELUJAH! – HOLY DAYS

Advent begins the church year. The Advent season consists of the four Sundays preceding Christmas. Blue or violet hangings and vestments are traditional, and the mood reflects a time of preparation and anticipation. The candle colors in the Advent wreaths for each of the Sundays have special meaning:

First week: The purple candle represents hope and prophecy.

Second week: Another purple candle stands for peace and preparation.

Third week: The pink candle represents joy and angels.

Fourth week: The final purple candle is the shepherds' candle.

The pink candle came from a tradition in which the Pope handed out roses. It is symbolic of those roses and much more practical today, when there are not enough popes, or roses, to go around. Some churches have returned to all purple candles, and some use blue. It probably has to do with matching the vestments.

Christmas or Christmas Eve: The center candle is always white, symbolizing the light of the world. Christmas begins on December 25 and lasts through the next two Sundays. The traditional color of the season is white. In very high churches there are two Red Letter Days during Christmastide: St. Stephen and St. John Apostle, December 26 and 27 respectively. The colors of these days are red. The Roman Catholic calendar is slightly different.

Epiphany, which follows, is also represented by the color white. It begins on January 6, the Night of the Kings, and runs to Ash Wednesday. The message of Epiphany includes the spreading of Christ's light to the world.

Lent begins with Ash Wednesday and ends on Easter eve, the night before Easter. Violet hangings are traditional, but some churches are using a sackcloth color. Some churches strip or veil the altar and use no flowers whatever during this season.

Easter hangings are white. On Good Friday—originally God's Friday—the hangings are black, for obvious reasons.

During Pentecost or Ordinary Time—the long period between Whitsunday (white Sunday), the seventh Sunday of Easter, and The Day of Pentecost and Advent—green hangings are traditional, since green is the symbolic color of renewal and fresh growth.

Special days or Red Letter Days are employed for special Saint's days, ordinations, confirmations and the Day of Pentecost. Red is an active color symbolizing zeal, martyrdom, commitment and faith.

Liturgical colors, the colors of the vestments and paraments—altar cloths, and the like—are violet for Advent and Lent; white for Christmas and Easter; and green for "Ordinary Time." The choice of flower color does not have to match the hangings, but there is drama in matching the frontal and vestments; or just as effectively, setting them off to best advantage with a strong contrast.

# INSPIRATIONS

# omega:
## RANDOM AND QUICK TIPS

- An apron with pockets is very helpful. A brightly colored cord to tie your clippers around your neck is a very good thing too.

- To open up a tight arrangement, put it in the warmest available place, feed it a little floral food or a shot of carbonated beverage. Place it in warm (not hot) water, and replace the warm water every twenty minutes for three times.

- To hold an arrangement that is maturing too fast, place it in the coolest place available.

- Keep your arrangement away from fans, vents and heaters as those drafts damage and dry out the flowers.

- Complete your arrangement the night before, if at all possible. Then you have time to refresh or pluck out any disappointing material.

- Handle the plant material as little as possible.

- Never pull out when you can clip out!

- Shape the Oasis as you wish; round and bevel corners, shape wet foam with wet hands. Cut it with monofilament or wire rather than a knife.

- A scar on a branch may be covered by smudging it with a bit of ash (easier to find when people smoked) but a brown marker will do.

- Have a large-lined garbage can, and keep your work area neat as you go along, or you will end up working in a jungle of wet slippery stems and foliage. Your clippers will be at the bottom of the pile, guaranteed.

- A lazy susan is helpful when arranging as it moves around and you don't; it keeps you working all the way around too, so the front does not get heavy.
- Draw an imaginary frame of the finished arrangement (cube) to determine size.
- Put some heavy material in the back, so that the design does not become front-heavy and over-full.
- If stems are weak, use a toothpick to make the insertion into the Oasis.
- Try to work at the same height as the one from which the finished arrangement will be viewed.
- Keep your cutting utensils sharp and your fingers out of their way.
- Measure twice, cut once. It is easier to make something shorter than longer. If you have cut something too short, you may insert the cut stem into a larger hollow stem and gain some height.
- Wishbone your flowers: This is my term, not technically correct, but descriptive. Many flowers, like mums, can be divided over and over again by separating the two outside stems and clipping in the center where they split; keep doing it and you get small flowers

on long stems which are perfect for adding filler at the top of an arrangement.

## ten or so other commandments:

- Thou shalt use Oasis only one time and place an individual stem into it only once. There is no need to jam a stem in hard.
- Thou shalt keep everything spotless, and keep those stems underwater which need to be underwater. Cutting underwater is even better. Glove thy hands for less cleanup of fingerprints.
- Thou shalt strip all extraneous foliage, especially that which is under the waterline. It is not a sin to replace natural foliage of a flower with another flower's foliage.
- Thou shalt not openly covet thy neighbor's clippers (but their

garden is ok); be sure to mark your own clippers.

- Thou shalt toss out droopy flowers and sub-par material. Bug bites and torn leaves neither mend nor do they grow back. Dead is dead. Recycle petals, however, if feasible.
- Thou shalt use only flowers thou hath conditioned for a minimum of two hours and preferably overnight.
- Thou shalt give fresh slanted cuts on all stems.
- Thou shalt use thy imagination; that is what it is for.
- Thou shalt have a good time; that is what time is for.
- Thou shalt praise thy fellow workers.
- Thou shalt be grateful for the opportunity to do the church's flowers.

In this book, I have listed some items by brand name, but endorse none in particular; they are all pretty much the same. New and improved products come along even as I write. I have utilized the books listed in the bibliography extensively and attempted to meld them into a light-hearted whole. I recommend any and all of them. I also used Google a whole lot. Some information was useful, and some was just really weird.

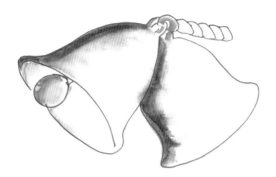

# postLude:

## FOR WHOM THE BELL TOLLS – A LIFE "ALTARING" EXPERIENCE

In this age when everything comes with a warning, I suppose even creating flower arrangements in church could be considered potentially hazardous. I will leave you with the story of a very frightening experience on the job, and you can evaluate the risk level for yourself:

I was working one Wednesday in the sacristy, preparing for the noon service which is held in the chapel every weekday. The sacristy is located between the chapel and the sanctuary. I went into the church for some silver piece, and a gust of wind slammed the door shut, locking me into the church. It was a good hour before the service, and for some reason, I had on my tightest pair of

panty hose, which were dissecting me, and I didn't have my reading glasses, so I couldn't even sit and read the prayer book. I thought about passing the time jogging up and down the aisle, but my skirt was too tight. I studied all the needlepoint in the kneelers. I was so bored, I even considered turning on the organ.

Then, it dawned on me that no one might come to look for me, as I had almost completed the set-up in the chapel. The vestry was on the other side, so I wouldn't hear when the priest came, and he wouldn't hear me knocking. To make matters worse, there was construction in the basement. They were making lots of clanging, and they couldn't hear me yelling through the vents. Fear trumped boredom. My options were to break out a Tiffany window, or sit until someone came to clean up or set up for Sunday services. It was Wednesday, remember. I envisioned searches and posters and starvation, if not dehydration. Martyrdom. As my frantic knocking went unheard, it suddenly came to me: Eureka! I remembered the bell. I went to the bell tower, hitched up my tight skirt and climbed the ladder to reach the rope bell pull. I tried to ring S O S (this church sits in the center of downtown Houston. The bell was pealing away for blocks, but after several attempts, no one on lunch break recognized the SOS). I figured constant ringing might bring somebody, if for anything just to get some peace and quiet!

The church offices were across the courtyard, and windows in Houston are hermetically sealed to keep the air-conditioning in. Finally, the Dean of the Cathedral, key in hand, came down to see who was making all that racket. He was most amused.

I was amused the next day.

So, wear comfortable clothes, look out for sudden gusts of wind, and go in peace to love and serve the Lord!

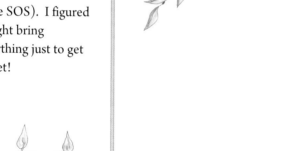

# INSPIRATIONS

# fLowers by coLor:

Some general tips on flower and plant material selection:

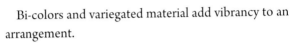

Bi-colors and variegated material add vibrancy to an arrangement.

Examples are some varieties of roses, snapdragons, iris, alstromeria, tulips, carnations, daffodils, geraniums, camellias, hydrangea, marigold, anemones, orchids, gloriosa lilies, etc.

Variegated holly, pittosporum, hosta, farfugium (formerly ligularia), privet, ti leaves, aspidistra, coleus, acuba, ivy, and other natural variegations can add depth and interest.

Fruits and vegetables offer variegation (and variety) too: Japanese eggplant, melons, beans, gourds, cabbages, kales, etc.

Note that hybridizing is going on as we speak; e.g., the rush to produce a truly black flower goes on and has been a popular though odd theme since the Dutch "tulipmania" in the sixteenth century. So this list will be increased endlessly and not just toward black; look for more purple purples and more chartreuse roses.

## true bLue

There are not too many true blue flowers and virtually none in the blue-yellow-cool range (cyanic); there are many in the red or xanthic range, tending toward purple. Some examples of blue are: delphinium, muscari (grape hyacinth), hyacinth, agapanthus, ecinops (globe thistle), salvia, aconitum (monk's hood, which is poisonous), ageratum, anemone, aster, campanula, centaurea (bachelor button), hydrangea, myosotis (forget-me-not) and statice. (Some foliages that may tend to blue are hosta and some ivies.)

### Righteous Red

Rose, carnation, tulip, poppy, kalanchoe, hypericum berries (new and wonderful; they last and come in lots of shades), hyacinth, heliconia, gloriosa lily, dianthus, gerbera daisies, montbrecia, bouvardia, freesia, anemone, anthurium, amaryllis, gladiolas, celosia (cockscomb), cyclamen, and torch ginger. Apples, lady apples, pomegranate, peppers, etc., add color from the grocery.

### Golden Yellow

Solidago (goldenrod) no, it is not an allergen; antirrhinum (snapdragon), kangaroo paw (anigozanthus), cymbidium and oncidium orchids, dianthus, carnation, marigold, eremerus (fox tail), forsythia, freesia, gerbera daises, zinnias, sunflowers, iris, gladiolas, oriental lily, calla lily, narcissus, ranunculus, tulip, chrysanthemum (pompom, button and Fuji), daisy, strawflower, yarrow, asters and many other composites. Squash, banana, lemon, peppers, apples.

### Pure White

Star of Bethlehem (ornithaligum), lilies, stock, gypsophila, gladiola, daisy, daisy mums, tulips, allium, anthurium, stock, chrysanthemum, convillaria (lily of the valley), delphinium (larkspur), dianthus, dendrobium, freesia, gerbera, hyacinth, iris, narcissus, rose, ranunculus, syringa (lilac), zinnia, agapanthus, allium, Queen Anne's lace, aster, delphinium, carnation, hydrangea, statice, matthiola (stock), peony, calla lily, cornus (dogwood), zephyranthus. Onions, mushrooms.

## Loving Lavender

Roses, allium, alstromeria, freesia, gladiolus, hyacinth, liatris (gay feather), carnations, limonium, orchids, syringa (lilac), trachelium, statice, German statice, peony, calla lily and of course lavender. In the store: Eggplant, ornamental kale, grapes, and beets.

## prayerful pinks

Roses, carnations, protea, ranunculus, phlox, nerine, peony, lily, sweet pea, hydrangea, gypsophila (baby's breath), gladiolus, delphinium, sweet William, larkspur, wax flower, mums, campanula, aster, amaryllis.

## p(r)each and orange

Alstromeria, gladiolus, lily, amaryllis, anthurium, mum, orchids, carnation, freesia, gerbera, rose, tulip, snapdragon, mum, dahlia, eremerus, stock, daffodil, zinnia, bird of paradise.

## glorious green

Carnations, button mums, 'Kermit' rose, foliages, hosta leaves, aspidistra, mums, ferns, ruscus, privet, amaranthus, bells of Ireland, anthurium, orchids, gladiolus, hypericum berry, palm, commodore, grass, alstromeria, galax, broom, liriope, asparagus fern, leeks, cabbage, asparagus spears, moss. Parsley works very well.

## marvelous metallic

There are also metallic foliages: silver such as protea, artemesia, eucalyptus, succulents (hen and chicks); silver evergreens, blue spruce, and lamb's ear; bronze: hypericum berry, fall foliage, maple, willow and other tree branches, chrysanthemum, daisy, snap dragon.

# flowers by season:

Flowers by Season is covered in Chapter 11—the colors indicate their seasonality with pastels and whites in the spring, strong yellow and purples and reds in the fall turning into metallic colors and the deep greens and berries of winter.

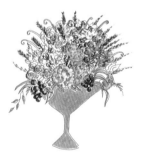

Spring flowers are the most delicate to condition as their blooming period is short; the fall flowers and summer flowers have a longer and stronger constitution. The evergreens are very hardy.

Standbys unlikely to ever let you down: carnations, statice, baby's breath, gladiolus, protea, alstromeria, galax leaves, aspidistra, kalanchoe, goldenrod and all heathers and statice. Succulents are always able to live without water for days.

Use with care: Orchids (need constant water), keep in the tubes if you can; roses (vulnerable to virus so prepare carefully and do not harm stem), wild carrot or Queen Anne's lace, lilac, and hydrangea (all are multi-headed flowers).

Heavenly scented: Roses, lilac, lily, carnation, dill, rosemary, citrus, some amaryllis, orchid, freesia, hyacinth, mock orange, sweet olive, mint, parsley and other herbs

Ungodly scented: Pear branches in flower, kale, cabbage, allium and all the onion family. Dirty water in the container.

Blacklock, Judith, *Teaching Yourself Flower Arranging*

Crocker, Ruth, *Elements and Principles of Design*

Ferguson, George, *Signs and Symbols in Christian Art*, Oxford Press

*Florist's Review Design School* publication, Florists Review

Gilliam, Hitomi, *Earth Man Spirit*

Garden Club of America, *Flower Show and Judges Guide*

Garden Club of Darien, *Petal Perfect*

Garden Club of Toronto, *Snippy Tips I and II*

Hamel, Esther Vera Mae, *Encyclopedia of Judging and Exhibiting*

Harwell, Dan, *Searching for Design*, Golden Spiral Press

Hynson, Sandra, *Flowers to the Glory of God*

Johnson, James L. and McKinley, William L., *Flowers: Creative Design*, Benz School of Design, Texas A&M University

Knowles, Reverend Archibald Campbell, *The Practice of Religion*, 1911

Lenden, Joanne, *Flowers for Bouquets*, Garden Field Florist

*Marysgardens@mgardens.com*

McKinley, William, *The Cut Flower Companion*

Sill, Gertrude Grace, *A Handbook of Symbols in Christian Art*, Collier Publishing

Taylor, Jean, *Flowers in Church*, Morehouse Barlow

Wetzler, Robert and Huntington, Helen, *Seasons and Symbols*, Augsburg Publishing House

# INSPIRATIONS